JESSE OWENS

Gold Medal Hero

Jim Gigliotti

STERLING

New York / London
www.sterlingpublishing.com/kids

STERLING and the distinctive Sterling logo are registered trademarks of
Sterling Publishing Co., Inc.

Library of Congress Cataloging-in-Publication Data
Gigliotti, Jim.
  Jesse Owens : gold medal hero / Jim Gigliotti.
    p. cm. — (Sterling biographies)
  Includes bibliographical references and index.
  ISBN 978-1-4027-7149-1 (hardcover) — ISBN 978-1-4027-6361-8 (pbk.) 1. Owens, Jesse,
1913–1980—Juvenile literature. 2. Track and field athletes—United States—Biography—Juvenile
literature. I. Title.
  GV697.O9G55 2010
  796.42092—dc22
  [B]
                                                                              2009024221

Lot #: 10 9 8 7 6 5 4 3 2 1
12/09

Published by Sterling Publishing Co., Inc.
387 Park Avenue South, New York, NY 10016
© 2010 by Jim Gigliotti

Distributed in Canada by Sterling Publishing
c/o Canadian Manda Group, 165 Dufferin Street
Toronto, Ontario, Canada M6K 3H6
Distributed in the United Kingdom by GMC Distribution Services
Castle Place, 166 High Street, Lewes, East Sussex, England BN7 1XU
Distributed in Australia by Capricorn Link (Australia) Pty. Ltd.
P.O. Box 704, Windsor, NSW 2756, Australia

Printed in China
All rights reserved

Sterling ISBN 978-1-4027-7149-1 (hardcover)
         ISBN 978-1-4027-6361-8 (paperback)

Image research by Jim Gigliotti and James Buckley, Jr.

For information about custom editions, special sales, premium and corporate
purchases, please contact Sterling Special Sales Department at 800-805-5489
or specialsales@sterlingpublishing.com.

Contents

Events in the Life of Jesse Owens

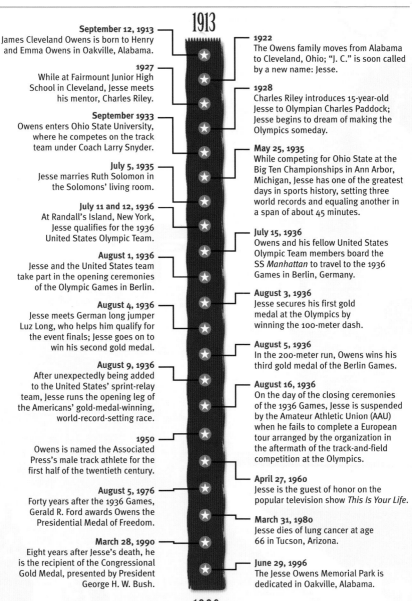

1913

September 12, 1913
James Cleveland Owens is born to Henry and Emma Owens in Oakville, Alabama.

1927
While at Fairmount Junior High School in Cleveland, Jesse meets his mentor, Charles Riley.

September 1933
Owens enters Ohio State University, where he competes on the track team under Coach Larry Snyder.

July 5, 1935
Jesse marries Ruth Solomon in the Solomons' living room.

July 11 and 12, 1936
At Randall's Island, New York, Jesse qualifies for the 1936 United States Olympic Team.

August 1, 1936
Jesse and the United States team take part in the opening ceremonies of the Olympic Games in Berlin.

August 4, 1936
Jesse meets German long jumper Luz Long, who helps him qualify for the event finals; Jesse goes on to win his second gold medal.

August 9, 1936
After unexpectedly being added to the United States' sprint-relay team, Jesse runs the opening leg of the Americans' gold-medal-winning, world-record-setting race.

1950
Owens is named the Associated Press's male track athlete for the first half of the twentieth century.

August 5, 1976
Forty years after the 1936 Games, Gerald R. Ford awards Owens the Presidential Medal of Freedom.

March 28, 1990
Eight years after Jesse's death, he is the recipient of the Congressional Gold Medal, presented by President George H. W. Bush.

1922
The Owens family moves from Alabama to Cleveland, Ohio; "J. C." is soon called by a new name: Jesse.

1928
Charles Riley introduces 15-year-old Jesse to Olympian Charles Paddock; Jesse begins to dream of making the Olympics someday.

May 25, 1935
While competing for Ohio State at the Big Ten Championships in Ann Arbor, Michigan, Jesse has one of the greatest days in sports history, setting three world records and equaling another in a span of about 45 minutes.

July 15, 1936
Owens and his fellow United States Olympic Team members board the SS *Manhattan* to travel to the 1936 Games in Berlin, Germany.

August 3, 1936
Jesse secures his first gold medal at the Olympics by winning the 100-meter dash.

August 5, 1936
In the 200-meter run, Owens wins his third gold medal of the Berlin Games.

August 16, 1936
On the day of the closing ceremonies of the 1936 Games, Jesse is suspended by the Amateur Athletic Union (AAU) when he fails to complete a European tour arranged by the organization in the aftermath of the track-and-field competition at the Olympics.

April 27, 1960
Jesse is the guest of honor on the popular television show *This Is Your Life*.

March 31, 1980
Jesse dies of lung cancer at age 66 in Tucson, Arizona.

June 29, 1996
The Jesse Owens Memorial Park is dedicated in Oakville, Alabama.

1996

Good Versus Evil

Finally he was willing to accept that all along he had been competing against Hitler.

—*Jeremy Schaap,* Triumph

Jesse Owens placed his toes in the small holes he had dug in the track at Berlin's Olympic Stadium. He rested his hands on the surface just behind the start line. His eyes focused on the finish line 100 meters away.

"On your marks," the starter said in German . . . Owens was America's best athlete, and he was favored to win the gold medal in this race at the 1936 Olympic Games. But the 100 meters had become more than just the Olympics' most famous event: it had become a chance to prove Adolf Hitler wrong. Hitler, Germany's leader, believed that African Americans, like Jesse Owens, were inferior to white people.

"Ready . . ." Jesse leaned his body forward. He knew that the race meant more than fulfilling his Olympic dream. It meant standing up for what was right and against what was wrong. His opponents in that battle weren't Olympic stars such as American Ralph Metcalfe in the 100 meters or even German Luz Long in the long jump. "He had gone to Berlin expecting to compete against Metcalfe and Long," author Jeremy Schaap wrote. "Finally, he was willing to accept that all along he had been competing against Hitler."

Pop! . . . The starter's gun went off. Jesse sprang out of his crouch and started to sprint.

CHAPTER 1

Humble Beginnings

I always loved running . . . because it was something you could do all by yourself, under your own power. You could go in any direction, seeking new sights just on the strength of your own feet and the courage of your own lungs.

It was a miracle that Jesse Owens was even alive in 1936, let alone stood as one of the world's greatest athletes. That's because he survived a childhood filled with disease and lacking in the basic necessities to combat illness. The things that many Americans take for granted, such as trips to the doctor and medicine when they get sick, were not always available in the early twentieth century—especially to poor black families in the South.

That was the world into which Jesse Owens was born in Oakville, Alabama, on September 12, 1913. Henry and Emma Owens, his parents, had already had twelve children before then. Three of them had died at birth, and the other nine included three girls—Ida, Josephine, and Lillie—and six boys—Prentice, Johnson, Henry, Ernest, Quincy, and Sylvester.

Henry and Emma didn't expect to have any more kids. So when Jesse—whom they named James Cleveland, "J. C." for short—came along, Emma called him her "gift child."

Oakville was a small town that was home to only a little more than 1,000 people at the time. They were mostly sharecroppers. Some of them were African American, like the Owens family, but mostly they were white. The sharecroppers picked cotton, as well as vegetables such as corn. The Owens family worked for a white man named Jim Cannon. He had several other sharecroppers who worked for him, too. The entire Owens family lived in a small, unheated three-room house. Cracks in the wooden walls let in cold air from outside. The beds for several of the kids consisted of blankets on the floor. They huddled close to keep warm on winter nights. As a kid J. C. was sick a lot, so he slept close to the stove to keep warm.

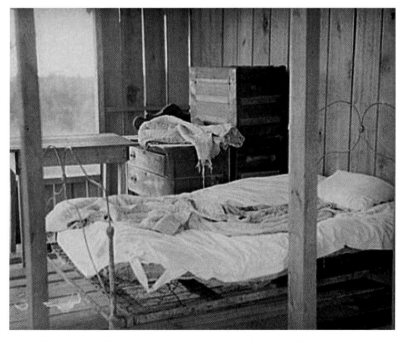

Cold air from the outside came through cracks in the wooden walls of the Owens home, just like the house in this picture from a sharecropper's home in the 1930s. In Jesse's case, though, he didn't even have a bed to sleep in. Instead, he and his siblings huddled on blankets on the floor.

Sharecropping

Sharecropping wasn't slave work, but economically it wasn't that much of a step up, either. Sharecroppers, who might be white or black (most of the sharecroppers who worked in Oakville alongside the Owens family, for instance, were white), worked the fields for the landowner. In exchange, sharecroppers got a home in which to live, perhaps a little equipment to work the field, and, sometimes, food to eat. The home was sometimes no more than a one- or two-room wooden shack. There was no electricity or running water.

At harvest time, each sharecropper and the landowner split the crops from the worker's particular plot of land. It might be an even split, or it might be unequal, in favor of the landowner. The sharecropper then had to pay back the rent and food out of his portion, too. By the time he was done, there usually wasn't much left. Any food left over had to be stored to get the family through the winter months. This left the sharecropper with no crops to sell, so there was little hope for saving money for a better life.

Sharecropping meant long, hard hours working in the fields. This photo of African Americans picking cotton is from the early 1900s, a few years before Jesse Owens was born in 1913.

Henry Owens dutifully did his job, always working hard for his family and for Mr. Cannon. But Henry wasn't filled with a lot of hope for the future. As the son of a slave, Henry had not received an education. He couldn't read or write. Sharecropping was the only work he knew, and he couldn't save any money doing that. He wanted his children to have more opportunities than he had.

Sharecropping was the only work he knew, and he couldn't save any money doing that.

So the Owens kids went to school when they could. It wasn't the same as it is now for most children. There wasn't a set schedule. Instead, they went to their local Baptist church when there was someone around to do some teaching—and when the crops didn't need picking. The whole family worked because Henry and Emma couldn't do it alone. When it was time to work the fields, all the kids took part. School had to wait.

Like the other kids, J. C. helped out when he could, but he was sick often, too. Every year, it seemed, he came down with severe bronchial sickness that left him drained and fatigued. Even more troubling, though, were boils, or pockets of infection, that J. C. developed on his skin. J. C.'s mom had to cut these out with a knife. The pain was almost unbearable—there was no medication for numbing the skin.

Near-Death Experience

The worst of the boils came when J. C. was only five years old. He noticed a bump on his chest the day after his birthday in 1918. Every day, the bump got bigger—and the pain got worse.

Emma and Henry had no doctor to call. There were doctors in Birmingham, but the big city was seventy-five miles away. And

This is a view of a well-kept, but sparsely furnished, sharecropper's home in Alabama in the 1930s. The Owens' kitchen would have looked similar.

even if they were able to get a doctor, the Owens family had no money to pay him.

Emma was worried. She had cut out the boils before, but never one this big. And besides, this one was close to J. C.'s heart. Despite her concern, Emma wasn't one to sit around and fret. Unlike her husband, she had a sense of hope and optimism for the future.

She knew what had to be done, so she did it. Late one night, after the other children were asleep, Emma woke up

J. C. It was time. "I'm going to take the bump out now, J. C.," she told him.

Emma had sterilized a kitchen knife by dunking it into kettles of boiling water on the stove. The heat was searing. When she started cutting out the boil, the pain was unbelievable. Young J. C. thought he knew pain, like the time that his foot had been caught in a trap set for an animal outside the house. But that was nothing compared to this. "Real pain is when you don't have any choice anymore whether to cry or not," he later said, "and then maybe you don't even cry because it wouldn't help."

At first J. C. cried, but the pain was so bad that he didn't even scream. Emma cut. She cut some more. Finally, the lump came out. She got all of it, too. But it left a hole more than an inch wide in J. C.'s chest. And he was bleeding—badly. It would not stop. "I was only five years old, but I knew I was dying," he later remembered.

Emma bandaged the wound as best as she could. That helped some, but she couldn't stop the bleeding entirely. Several nights later, J. C. woke up in the middle of the night. He heard his dad, who was a deacon at the same Baptist church where J. C. later would go to school, praying outside. J. C. dragged himself out the door and joined him. "Pray, James Cleveland," his dad told him. "Pray."

By the time that Henry carried J. C. back into the house, the bleeding had stopped. Henry and Emma's "gift child" soon made a full recovery.

Always on the Move

Late in his life, Jesse Owens became a popular speaker. He traveled all over the country talking about his experiences to a

This is an outside look at the family's Alabama home as depicted at the Jesse Owens Museum.

wide variety of audiences. He told the story of his near-death experience when he was just five years old in speech after speech.

It might sound as if J. C. had a difficult or an unhappy childhood. He grew up without any running water or electricity, without even a radio. The Owens family never had much money, either. The kids had one shirt to wear to church on Sundays, and one for the rest of the week. They ate meat only to celebrate birthdays, or Christmas and Easter. Usually, they ate fruits and vegetables, beans, and jams.

But J. C. didn't feel like anything was missing. He was sick a lot, which was no fun. And the family couldn't pay for any medicine to make him feel better. Except for that, though, J. C. was happy. For one thing, he didn't know any different life.

"We used to have a lot of fun," he said. "We never had any problems. We always ate. The fact that we didn't have steak? Who had steak?"

Steak was a luxury to people of modest means. No one among J. C.'s friends had steak every night for dinner. J. C. had plenty of friends to keep him busy. He had friends at school and in the town. He had lots of brothers and sisters, too, for companionship. And even though he didn't have toys, he had his imagination—and his legs.

"I always loved running," he said. "I loved it because it was something you could do all by yourself, under your own power. You could go in any direction, seeking new sights just on the strength of your own feet and the courage of your own lungs."

J. C.'s running could take him just about anywhere in Oakville. There were places that his legs couldn't take him, though—places where African Americans were not granted the same access as other Americans. Though President Abraham Lincoln's Emancipation Proclamation freed slaves in ten Confederate states in 1863, there continued to be a lot of **bigotry** against African Americans in the South.

Besides having to overcome these existing prejudices, many African Americans there were put out of work by a small beetle called the boll weevil. By the 1920s, the boll weevil had destroyed cotton crops throughout the region.

Without any opportunities in Oakville, it was time to try something else.

Hundreds of thousands of African Americans in the South moved to the North between 1910 and 1930. The Owens family was among them. Without any opportunities in Oakville, it was time to try something else.

The Emancipation Proclamation

During the American Civil War, which was lasted from 1861 to 1865, Union states (the North) and Confederate states (the South) fought over the issue of slavery. The Union wanted to **abolish** slavery, but the Confederacy remained in favor of the practice.

On January 1, 1863, President Abraham Lincoln's Emancipation Proclamation declared that slaves in ten Confederate states were free. Technically, Lincoln had no power over those states because they had left the Union. But the Proclamation still was a powerful tool because it committed the Union to ending slavery, and it laid the groundwork for the Thirteenth Amendment, which officially abolished slavery. That amendment was ratified, or approved, in December of 1865.

African Americans were free, but they still had a long road to equality. That was especially true in the South, where J. C. was born only fifty years after the Emancipation Proclamation took effect, and even fewer than that since the Thirteenth Amendment had been ratified.

The Emancipation Proclamation is one of the United States' most important historical documents. This lithograph with the Proclamation's text on it was created in 1888.

CHAPTER 2

Northern Exposure

It's gonna take us to a better life.

—Emma Owens

One day late in 1922, Henry and Emma Owens broke the news to their children. Emma told them to pack up their things. Put your "belongings together and tie them up tight," she said to them.

"Where are we gonna go, Momma?" J. C. asked.

"We're goin' on a train," his mom said.

Like tens of thousands of other black families in the South in the 1920s, the Owens family was heading to the North. There were factories in the North, which meant there were jobs. There was affordable housing in the North, too, which meant the large family didn't have to live in such a small and crowded house. And there was less racial prejudice in the North—for the most part.

The family already had sent J. C.'s oldest sister, Lillie, to Cleveland, Ohio, to live with relatives there. Lillie found a job, got married, and wrote to the family back in Alabama. "I told them the opportunities were better there," she later said about Cleveland.

Henry couldn't read Lillie's words, but Emma could. Henry didn't grasp that moving meant better opportunities for the family, either, but Emma did. She was on board with the idea right away. She knew there was something better for her and her family out there. Henry wasn't so sure. He figured they had food on the table as things were.

This is what Public Square in downtown Cleveland looked like in 1916, shortly before the Owens family moved there from Alabama.

"We'd never make it," J. C. overheard his dad telling his mother. "We'd starve." The way Henry saw it, things sure weren't ever going to get any better where they were—but they weren't likely to get any worse, either.

It took some doing, but Emma finally convinced Henry that they had to make the move. And so the Owens family found themselves waiting on a train platform in Alabama, with everything they owned—which wasn't much—in tow.

"And where's the train gonna take us, Momma?" J. C. asked Emma.

"It's gonna take us to a better life," she said.

New Home, New Name

The train took the Owens family to meet up with Lillie in Cleveland. There, they rented a house in a poor neighborhood with families from lots of different backgrounds: black and white, American and immigrant.

Young J. C. enrolled in Bolton Elementary School. There were no crops to pick, so for the first time in his life, he began going to school every day. For the first time in his life, too, he found himself in a mixed school in Cleveland: black kids sitting next to white kids. He might have been a little bit nervous the first day, when his new teacher called on him.

For the first time in his life, too, he found himself in a mixed school in Cleveland: black kids sitting next to white kids.

"What is your name?" she asked the new student.

"J. C.," Owens replied, although a bit too fast.

"Jesse?" she said.

"No, ma'am. It's J. C."—again, too fast. Again, the teacher misunderstood.

"Well, your name is Jesse, isn't it?"

The nine-year-old was as shy as he was nervous, so he agreed. "Yes, ma'am," he said. So his name was Jesse from that day on.

Jesse Owens not only was in a new school in a new city, but now he had a new name, too.

Dressed for Success

Cleveland did provide the Owens family with more opportunities. The younger children went to school more regularly than they ever had in Alabama, while the older children went to work. Henry and a couple of his sons found employment

This photo shows a busy steel mill in Cleveland in 1926. Henry Owens and a couple of Jesse's brothers went to work in such a place.

The Steel Mill

A steel mill is where iron ore (rocks and minerals from which iron can be extracted) is processed into steel, which can then be used in industry.

Steel mills were an important part of the economy in Ohio in the late nineteenth and early twentieth centuries. Furnaces in Ohio had produced iron for many years, then quickly adopted new technology when steel production was introduced after the American Civil War (which ended in 1865). Because steel is stronger and more malleable (meaning it can be shaped and extended) than iron, it could be used for building structures such as skyscrapers and bridges. That helped the industry experience rapid growth until the Great Depression of the 1930s, when almost all facets of the American economy suffered. Steel mills bounced back again when the United States entered World War II in 1941. The military needed steel in the production of gun, ships, and tanks.

Work in the mills was difficult and sometimes dangerous, but it was steady employment—and it kept food on the table.

in a steel mill. Emma and her daughters cleaned houses. All of the Owens family members were good workers because they were all used to working hard in the fields. Money wasn't exactly flowing, but there was some of it—enough for everyone to buy another shirt or dress for during the week, and maybe to put meat on the table for Sunday evenings.

Jesse may not have had to work in the fields anymore, and he was going to school every day, but he still did his part to help out the family. While his sister Lillie worked, he baby-sat for her two kids—he was the "best baby-sitter I ever had," she said many years later—and he worked at a variety of other jobs as well.

One was at Tony's Shoe Repair in Cleveland. Jesse did lots of work there, from cleaning up to shining shoes. He gave some of the money to his family to help buy food, and he saved some, too. He saved enough to buy Lillie a dress.

Clothes were always important to Jesse. Maybe he simply appreciated them more because he had had so little clothing growing up. Even when he got older and was known the world round, he never took clothes for granted. Maybe new clothes made him feel good about how far he had come. Whatever the reason, throughout his adult life, Jesse always dressed well—and made sure his family did, too.

Jesse always was a stylish dresser. This photo is from 1936, as he hurries to catch a train.

Lasting Relationships

After Bolton Elementary School, Jesse attended Fairmount Junior High School in Cleveland. At Fairmount, he met several people who would help shape the rest of his life. One of them was David Albritton, a friend his age.

David was from Danville, Alabama, only miles from Jesse's hometown of Oakville. David, also African American, was born in April 1913, just five months earlier than Jesse. And just as the Owens family had done, the Albritton family moved north from Alabama in search of better opportunities. Jesse and David became fast friends, and they remained friends for the rest of Jesse's life. The two of them hung out at Fairmount, and later were on the track team together at East Technical High School and at Ohio State University.

Jesse also met his future wife, Ruth, at Fairmount. "I fell in love with her some the first time we ever talked," he remembered many years later. Ruth, whose full name was Minnie Ruth Solomon, came from a poor family, too, but from the way she talked, dressed, and carried herself, it didn't seem that way to Jesse.

Ruth was two years younger than Jesse, who was older than most of his classmates. Because of his lack of schooling in Alabama, Jesse was several grades behind most of the other kids his age. But Ruth was charmed by Jesse's ready smile and easygoing personality. She liked that he was humble and even a little shy. The two began dating.

With new friends, a new sweetheart, and a new home, there was a lot going on in Jesse's life in the late 1920s. But when he wasn't working at the shoe repair shop or delivering groceries or pumping gas at the local service station, he loved to play, just like any other fifteen-year-old boy. He was pretty good at

David Albritton (1913–1994)

David Albritton, who forged a lifelong friendship with Jesse Owens, is a member of the National Track & Field Hall of Fame. Albritton was a terrific all-around athlete who was good at basketball and boxing as well as track and field.

Albritton was one of the first high jumpers to use the straddle technique. Straddle jumpers approach the bar at an angle and take off on their inside foot, then swing their other foot over the bar, rotating their torso over it. Before Albritton, the most successful jumpers used a "Western roll" that took them over the bar sideways. Today, almost all of the best high jumpers use the "Fosbury Flop," with their back to the bar.

Albritton and Cornelius Johnson were America's top two high jumpers in 1936. They each jumped a world-record height of 6 feet 9¾ inches at the Olympic Trials that year. At the Games in Berlin, Germany, Johnson won the gold medal, while Albritton took the silver.

After the Olympics, Albritton continued to compete at Ohio State University, and he won National Collegiate Athletic Association (NCAA) championships in both 1937 and 1938 in the high jump. He later became a politician who served in the Ohio House of Representatives.

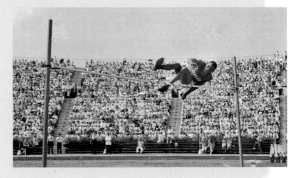

David Albritton shows off his straddle technique while competing in the high jump at the United States Olympic Trials in 1936.

Jesse is pictured as a gas station attendant. He worked several jobs during his high school and college years to help his family financially.

basketball, which he liked to play with his friend David, but he was best at running. He could run faster than anybody else he knew—no one else was even close.

One day in 1927, Jesse and his friends ran a race about 100 yards long. Charles Riley, the gym teacher at Fairmount, saw Jesse easily win the race. That was no big deal. But this time, it seemed almost as if the other kids had barely taken off by the time Jesse flew across the finish line. Mr. Riley knew that Jesse was fast. But he didn't realize he was that fast!

CHAPTER 3

Coach and Mentor

If this lad takes track seriously, he will be in the Olympics someday.
— *Charles Riley*

Charles Riley would go on to become one of the biggest influences in Jesse Owens's life. Riley had seen Jesse playing with the other boys at Fairmount. He saw a young man who was eager to learn and eager to please—and one with exceptional athletic ability. But he also saw that Jesse was unpolished, and would need some coaching if he wanted to fulfill his athletic potential.

So one day Riley stopped to talk to Jesse. "How'd you like to be on the track team when you get to high school?" he asked.

Of course Jesse would! He loved nothing more than to run. He also wanted very much to be liked by others, and here was a chance to be part of a team and to make new friends. But high school was still a couple of years away, and Jesse had a lot to learn about running. That would mean doing a lot more than the work Riley did with the other kids in gym class. It would mean meeting with the coach after school to run and do other exercises.

This was not a problem—Riley was willing, and Jesse was able. It was all set. "Well then, see you tomorrow, Jesse," Riley said.

Track and Field

"Track and field" is the collective term applied to a series of running, jumping, and throwing events. In the Olympic Games, the category is commonly called "athletics."

Running events vary greatly in distance, from short (as few as 50 meters in indoor races) to long (the steeplechase, which includes various obstacles on the track, is 3,000 meters). Jumping events include the long jump, high jump, triple jump, and pole vault. Throwing events include the discus, hammer, javelin, and shot put.

Jesse Owens was a sprinter, meaning he ran short races, up to 220 yards. That included a portion of the 400-meter relay race. This race is usually written as the "4 × 100 meter relay," meaning each of four competitors on the same team runs 100 meters, with a baton passed from runner to runner. (If the baton is dropped, the team is disqualified.)

In team track-and-field meets, competitors are awarded points for their finish in different events. Scoring varies according to the rules of a particular competition. In a typical championship meet, though, with many teams competing, the winner earns ten points for his squad, and second place gets eight points. Six to eight competitors can earn at least one point.

Jesse could hardly wait. There was only one problem. Jesse was so excited to get started that he forgot he worked after school! Some days it was at the shoe repair shop. A couple of days a week, he delivered groceries. Another day, he worked at a greenhouse. He couldn't give up those jobs. His family needed the money.

Riley understood. The solution was simple. "You'll run before school, won't you?" he asked.

The Odd Couple

So every morning before school, Jesse got up to run. And jump. And twist. And turn. And bend. Before Jesse started training with Riley, running just meant going from Point A to Point B as fast as his legs could take him. He had never had any formal training. But Riley taught Jesse about technique. He taught him the **fundamentals** of running, such as how to keep the body upright with a slight lean forward, and the proper way to stretch before and after races. He also taught him about the mental parts of running, such as focus and concentration. All of that helped Jesse get from Point A to Point B even faster than before.

Riley became Jesse's **mentor** not only on the track, but off the track, too. It was an unusual pairing. Riley was white; Jesse was black. Riley was about fifty years old when he met Jesse; the boy was only fifteen. And he had never had a white man take a sincere interest in his well-being.

Riley had several children of his own; Jesse, of course, had his own father. But Riley treated Jesse like he was a member of his own family. Jesse and Riley often had breakfast together before

Riley became Jesse's mentor not only on the track, but off the track, too.

or after their workouts. They talked about running, but they talked about life, too. "He trained me to become a man as well as an athlete," Jesse said. Young Owens often ate dinner over at the Riley house. On weekends, Riley would drive over to Jesse's house. The two would head off in Riley's car and talk about how things were going at school or what Jesse's hopes were for the future. "Coach Riley taught me to behave," Jesse said. "His influence on me and many other boys kept us out of trouble."

Years later, lots of kids would say the same thing about Jesse Owens. As an adult, he often worked with young people while on the Illinois State Athletic Commission and in other jobs. "A boy interested in sports won't get into trouble," he believed.

That was one way that Jesse, who never forgot those days traveling around in Riley's old Model T Ford, honored his mentor. He did it in another, more personal, way, too: "After the 1936 Olympics, Jesse came back and went to work," Coach Riley

These Model-Ts rolled off the Ford assembly line in 1925. Charles Riley and Jesse spent many hours in just such a car, traveling to and from competitions and talking about running and about life.

recalled, "and one of the first things that he did was to buy me a new car."

To the Track

One day when Jesse was still in junior high school, as he liked to recall many years later, Riley said they would spend a Saturday afternoon watching the "best runners in the whole world." Jesse had no idea what that meant until they pulled up to the local racetrack: they were there to see the horses run.

Jesse and Mr. Riley (as Jesse usually called him, even in later years) pulled into the parking lot. They walked past the betting booths and made their way through the spectators poring over the *Daily Racing Form*. This newspaper lists the horses that are racing that day and gives lots of statistics to help the fans who want to place a bet. But Jesse and Mr. Riley weren't there to gamble. Instead, they took a position right on the rail so they could watch the horses up close.

Jesse was amazed by what he saw. Race after race he watched the huge animals run with incredible power and speed around the track. And yet they looked as if they were hardly trying at all.

"Do you know why the best horses make it look so easy?" Mr. Riley asked Jesse. "Because the determination is all on the inside, where no one can see it."

Mr. Riley didn't like what he had seen in some of Jesse's earliest races. He felt like Jesse

> *Race after race he watched the huge animals run with incredible power and speed around the track. And yet they looked as if they were hardly trying at all.*

was showing how hard he was trying with his facial expressions and his mannerisms. He didn't want Jesse putting on a big

For the rest of his life, Jesse recalled the lessons he learned watching horses race. These horses are racing at Belmont Park in New York in 1929—just about the time that Charles Riley took a teenaged Owens to the track.

show for the other runners and the spectators. Trying to show determination wasn't the same as having real determination. It had to be on the inside, just as it was with the horses.

After that, Jesse kept that in mind every time he ran. The apparent ease of his effort became the hallmark of his racing style.

"I never saw a man run with such ease," said Frank Wykoff, a famous sprint champion himself who was a gold medalist in three consecutive Olympics beginning in 1928. "He doesn't appear to be running fast at all. He isn't half trying, yet he gets there first."

"He is the picture of relaxed ease as he sprints," journalist Jesse Abramson wrote in the *New York Herald Tribune*. "He never shows any apparent effort. He always appears able to do better."

"He did it all so easily," said Ken Doherty, who was an assistant coach at the University of Michigan, Ohio State's **archrival**, when Jesse was in college, "and wouldn't it be great when he really tried?"

Doherty was just joking, of course. Jesse was trying as hard as he could. He simply had learned his lesson from Coach Riley.

Another area Coach Riley worked long and hard with Jesse on were on his starts. In Owens's early days of running, starting blocks were not used. Instead, Jesse and the other runners dug small holes into the track to give them a little help pushing off at the start. Other runners utilized that to better advantage than Jesse did, though. He was not the best at starting a race—but he was the best at finishing a race.

One common observation was that Jesse's feet hardly seemed to touch the track when he ran. That came from Mr. Riley's lessons, too. "Jesse, you just make believe that track's a red-hot stove lid and let your feet touch it as little as possible," he said. "Each foot of that pair you've got should try to beat the other one to it." Other times, Coach Riley told Jesse "to always run as if you were dancing on hot coals."

A New Goal

In 1928, Riley introduced fifteen-year-old Jesse Owens to Charles Paddock, then the "World's Fastest Human." (The World's Fastest Human is the nickname given to the reigning record holder in the 100-meter dash.) This meeting turned out

Starting Blocks

When Jesse Owens first began competing, runners dug their own starting holes. They were given a small trowel and got down on their hands and knees before a race to make small indentations in the cinder track. This would not be possible on today's hard-rubber surfaces! Instead, today's runners have the benefit of a crisp, clean getaway because of starting blocks attached to the track itself.

Actually, an early form of running blocks first appeared in the late 1920s. Some reports say they were invented by a couple of American coaches, others say by an Australian runner named Charlie Booth (1903–2008). In either case, the reason probably had less to do with a quick getaway than it did with preserving the tracks on which runners practiced and competed.

Still, starting blocks were considered an illegal aid to runners and were not permitted in international competition until 1937. That year, they were officially allowed by the International Association of Athletics Federations. However, starting blocks were not used in the Olympics until 1948.

This runner is set to break from the starting blocks. For most of his career, Jesse did not have that advantage.

Meeting Charles Paddock helped Jesse forge his Olympic dream. Paddock shows off his unique running style in this photograph from 1931.

to have a profound impact on Jesse's life. Paddock became his sporting idol.

Riley had arranged for the Olympic star to talk to the kids at Fairmount. Afterward, Riley, Paddock, and Owens met in the coach's office. Jesse was in awe. In the 1920 Olympics in Belgium, Paddock had won a gold medal in the 100 meters and a silver medal in the 200 meters. Then he had led the United States to a gold medal in the 4 × 100 meter relay. He added a silver medal in the 200 meters in Paris four years later.

Jesse may not have even been aware of the Olympics when Paddock first started winning his medals, but he learned quickly.

The Olympic Games

The modern Olympic Games were still a relatively new phenomenon in Jesse Owens's youth. The ancient Olympics, however, were first held in Greece in 776 BCE, but eventually were banned more than 1,000 years later by a Roman emperor in 393 CE.

A French teacher named Pierre de Coubertin organized and reintroduced the games—the modern Olympic Games—in Athens in 1896. It was de Coubertin's dream to revive the international competition as a means of promoting goodwill among all nations.

That year, eighty-one athletes from thirteen countries joined more than two hundred participants from Greece in the Olympics. Ever since, the Summer Olympics have been held every four years (except for the war years of 1916, 1940, and 1944). The first Winter Olympics were held in 1924. In 1994, the Winter Games took place only two years after the previous Games, then got back to the regular four-year schedule. This way, the Summer Olympics and the Winter Olympics are now held in different even-numbered years.

Baron Pierre de Coubertin is the father of the modern Olympics. He dreamed of reprising the Games of ancient Greece.

Beyond the medals, too, Paddock was a *star*. He was one of the first athletes to take his Olympic fame and use it to make money in other areas. He acted in the movies, wrote books and articles, and became a newspaper executive.

And suddenly, not only was Jesse in the same room as the great Charles Paddock, but Mr. Riley was saying how Jesse might one day follow in Paddock's footsteps! "If this lad takes track seriously," Riley told Paddock, "he will be in the Olympics someday."

Coach Riley had enough confidence in Jesse to say something like that to one of the world's greatest Olympians. That gave Jesse a bolt of confidence. "Coach Riley told me that I could be like this man," Jesse said. "He said it would take work, and a great deal of effort. Those are the things that I live by."

The Olympics were no longer something Jesse had only heard about. Now they were a goal.

The Olympics were no longer something Jesse had only heard about. Now they were a goal. Could the sharecropper's son, the inexperienced Cleveland schoolboy, be in the Olympic Games someday?

CHAPTER 4

School Days

The great Jesse Owens. I want to know all about you.
—Larry Snyder

After Fairmount Junior High, Jesse entered East Technical High School in the fall that he turned seventeen years old. At East Tech, it looked as if he would have to get used to a new track coach. That was okay with Jesse. He knew he couldn't train with Coach Riley all his life. But the East Tech track coach, a recent college graduate named Edgar Weil, was young and inexperienced, and he needed help. So he turned to . . . Charles Riley. After all, Riley had already worked with some of the kids at Fairmount, including, of course, Jesse Owens.

Riley was delighted to help, and he and Jesse were reunited. David Albritton competed on

Jesse attended East Technical High School in Cleveland after Fairmount Junior High. He, along with his friend David Albritton, helped East Tech build a powerful track squad.

the same team, too. He was getting to be an accomplished high jumper. Owens and Albritton combined to help give East Tech a **formidable** track-and-field team.

By this time, Jesse was the only member of his family still in school. Each of the others had been forced to drop out to make whatever money he or she could to help the family. The United States was in the midst of the Great Depression, and money was very tight for almost everyone. The Owens family needed as many of its members as possible to be working as much as they could in order to make ends meet. Perhaps Jesse was allowed to stay in school because he was the youngest. Or perhaps it was because his boundless energy enabled him to work at various jobs even after his schoolwork and his track practice were done for the day.

Jesse was very popular at East Tech. He was still soft-spoken and mild-mannered, but his athletic ability gave him a quiet confidence. By his senior year, he was captain of the track team, as well as president of the student council. The girls adored him, although he was in love only with Ruth.

Word about Jesse's accomplishments on the track quickly spread. Everywhere he competed, thousands of spectators turned out to cheer him on. He rarely disappointed them. Out of 79 races while at East Tech, Jesse won 75.

In June 1932, near the end of Jesse's junior year in high school, he ran the 100-meter dash in 10.3 seconds in a meet in Cleveland. That equaled the world record held at the time by Canada's Percy Williams. Owens's mark didn't count as a world record because there was a **tailwind**. (In current track-and-field rules, the maximum tailwind allowed for a record to be counted is 2.0 meters per second. By putting a limit on the wind speed allowed, track experts can compare equal

The Great Depression

The Great Depression was a decade-long period of economic problems that gripped the United States and much of the rest of the world during the 1930s. It began with a shocking drop in the **stock market**—the Wall Street crash—on "Black Tuesday," October 24, 1929.

For the next ten years, the United States struggled with a rise in unemployment and a decline in business. Many people who had been prosperous in the 1920s suddenly lost their jobs, and then their homes. Their entire life savings were wiped out almost overnight. Banks and other businesses failed.

With the beginning of World War II in 1939, the United States (although it did not officially enter the war until 1941) began heavy military spending. That, and the drafting of millions of men into the armed forces, helped spur the economy and lower unemployment. Money had to be spent to make planes and ships and ammunition, and men and women had to be hired to produce them. Many of the New Deal policies of President Franklin Delano Roosevelt in the 1930s also are credited with helping the United States recover from the Great Depression.

Military spending in the late 1930s and early 1940s helped spur the U.S. economy. In this photograph from 1943, a woman works on the landing gear of a World War II dive-bomber.

Jesse crosses the finish line to win a 220-yard race while competing for East Tech. He was almost unbeatable in his time at the school, with 75 victories in 79 races.

conditions.) That rule may have prevented Jesse from setting the world record, but it didn't keep his performance from qualifying him for the regional Olympic Trials in Evanston, Illinois, the following week.

The Olympic Games were slated to be held in Los Angeles, California, in August 1932. Only four years earlier, Jesse had determined that he would be in the Olympics one day. Was that day already here?

No, it wasn't. For the first time in his life, Jesse was overmatched on the track. He was only eighteen years old, and wide-eyed in the company of world-class stars. He was not big enough or strong enough yet, and to compound that, he tried too hard. He didn't come close to moving on to the final Olympic Trials, let alone the Games themselves.

Jesse was so disappointed in his failure at the regional qualifying that he figured Riley would be ashamed to see him. That couldn't have been further from the truth, of course. Coach Riley knew, and Jesse would soon realize, that his time would come.

Bouncing Back

Like all great athletes can do, Jesse quickly put the disappointment of the preliminary Olympic Trials behind him. He knew that he had to get bigger and stronger. And he knew that mentally, he had to better handle being in that situation. He couldn't be awed by great athletes around him. He needed to stay focused. Those were things he could work on, though. And he had four years to do it before the 1936 Games.

Like all great athletes can do, Jesse quickly put the disappointment of the preliminary Olympic Trials behind him.

So Jesse went back to East Tech to complete his senior year. Before that, however, came two more significant events, one off the track and one on it. Off the track, he became a father when Ruth gave birth to the couple's first daughter. Gloria Shirley Owens was born on August 8, 1932. Jesse was only eighteen years old; Ruth was just sixteen. Ruth's mother took care of the baby much of the time.

Less than two weeks later, Jesse was delighted to be invited to compete in a meet in Cleveland. More than twenty athletes in the meet had just participated in the Olympics in Los Angeles. After his disappointment at the Olympic Trials, Jesse was glad for the chance to show what he was capable of accomplishing in what the International News Service called the "Little Olympics."

This was at a time when track and field was much more popular than it is now. Baseball was America's most popular sport, and college football and boxing had big followings, too. But the National Football League (NFL) was very young, and would not really take hold on the sporting scene until the arrival of widespread television. The National Basketball Association (NBA) was still more than a decade away from beginning. The National Hockey League (NHL) was played in only a handful of cities. Track and field not only was popular, but it was also the biggest sport in the Olympic Games, which had held its closing ceremonies just seven days earlier. And without television, the only way that fans could see their favorite stars—aside from an occasional **newsreel** clip at the local movie theater—was in person.

More than 50,000 fans flocked to the invitational meet at Municipal Stadium. Jesse put on a show for the hometown spectators, many of whom were there to see him run and, according to newspaper accounts, gave him thunderous ovations. He won the 100- and 220-yard dashes, and finished second only to Edward Gordon, an American who had won the Olympic gold medal, in the long jump.

Ten months later, in June 1933, Jesse closed his high school career with a fantastic performance in the top high school competition of the year, the National Interscholastic Championships in Chicago, Illinois. He scored 30 of East Tech's winning 54 points all by himself. He tied the world record by running the 100-yard dash in 9.4 seconds, and set national high-school marks in the 220-yard dash (20.7 seconds) and in the long jump (24 feet 9 inches).

Jesse proudly shows his mom the medals that he won at the National Interscholastic Championships in Chicago in 1933.

Off to "Kolledge"

In Columbus, Ohio, Larry Snyder, the head track coach at Ohio State University, pored over the results of that interscholastic meet in Chicago. He had never met Jesse Owens, but he sure knew who Owens was. Like every other coach at every other big-time college program, Snyder wanted the nation's best high-school track athlete to compete at his school starting in the fall of 1933.

Snyder didn't figure his chances were great, however. Some Ohio State **boosters** would do their best to convince Jesse to attend the school, as it was done in those days, but Ohio State had a reputation for racial intolerance. Black newspapers throughout the Midwest were imploring Jesse to pick a school that was friendlier to African Americans.

Dozens of schools offered Jesse a scholarship, which means the school will pay for school fees and books, and sometimes more. Jesse almost decided on the University of Michigan. Ann Arbor, Michigan, where the school was located, had a reputation for being fairer to African Americans than Columbus, home of Ohio State. Plus, Michigan reportedly offered Jesse's dad a job taking care of an apartment building.

In the end, though, Jesse settled on Ohio State. Years later, he credited Coach Riley with helping steer him to that university, although some accounts indicate that his old coach wanted Jesse to go to Michigan. Still, Riley knew that Jesse would be in good hands at Ohio State with Coach Snyder.

The first time Owens joined Coach Snyder in his office at Ohio State was the first time the two met. "The great Jesse Owens," Snyder said. "I want to know all about you."

Ohio State was close to home, it had the best track-and-field program in the state, and it offered Jesse a job operating an elevator in the State House in Columbus. His parents had no complaints about their son's choice, but black

Jesse poses in his Ohio State track uniform. He attended the university after graduating from East Tech in 1933.

newspapers weren't happy about it. "Many and long were the outcries against his decision," one newspaper story said a couple of years later.

Jesse, though, had his eye on the Olympics, not on making any political statements. The job at the State House was perfect for him. Because it was at night and only occasionally involved transporting members of the building's cleaning crew, it allowed Jesse the time and a quiet place to keep up with his studies.

Jesse studied hard at Ohio State, but the fact that he was in college at all was a bit of a surprise, and had more to do with his athletic ability than his academic skills. School was difficult for Jesse. He wrote in his memoirs that, as a youngster, he often had dreamed of one day going to "kolledge." He had only occasionally gone to school back in Alabama. When he got to high school in Cleveland, the emphasis was more on trade skills such as welding and construction, and less on reading and writing. He was not adequately prepared to meet the academic challenges that awaited him at the university.

Perhaps Jesse's best education at Ohio State came once a week, when Coach Snyder took him to local schools and organizations to talk about the university. Jesse earned extra spending money for giving these talks, but they also gave him a chance to work on his speaking skills. Over time, he became an excellent public speaker. Later in his life, he was in constant demand to talk to groups, which he did with passion and joy.

CHAPTER 5

One Day in May

I think it was the greatest performance any athlete will ever do in any sport.

—Red Simmons

Columbus, Ohio, isn't very far from Cleveland—only about a two-and-a-half-hour drive. For Jesse Owens, though, as he began life as a college student at Ohio State, it might as well have been in a different country altogether.

That's because, for the first time, Jesse was out on his own. He no longer had his brothers and sisters—and sometimes their spouses and children—living under the same roof with him. He no longer had his mom doting on him, cooking his meals and ironing his clothes every morning before school. And he no longer had Coach Riley with him on the track every day, offering encouragement about his running and advice about life. He was still dating Ruth, but it was a long-distance relationship: she was still in Cleveland.

As it turned out, Columbus's reputation for hostility to African Americans proved to be accurate. Jesse couldn't live near campus; he and several other black athletes shared an apartment off campus. They couldn't eat at the same college hot spots as the white athletes. Even the elevator Jesse operated was a freight elevator located in the back of the building—the white athletes operated the passenger elevator in the front of the

This photograph is of Orton Hall on the Ohio State campus. Jesse first entered the school in the fall of 1933.

building. And only about one in every twenty students at Ohio State was African American.

However, Larry Snyder, the school's track-and-field coach, did his best to make Jesse feel welcome on campus. Maybe that was out of a sense of fairness to all of his athletes regardless of the color of their skin, or maybe it was simply because, like all coaches, he wanted to win—and Jesse and other black athletes on the squad, such as Jesse's friend David Albritton, gave him the best chance of winning.

It helped, too, that Jesse and Coach Snyder hit it off right away. They genuinely seemed to like each other, and Snyder quickly helped fill the void left by Jesse's far-off mentor, Mr. Riley.

Jesse stands with Larry Snyder, the coach of Ohio State's track team. Snyder had never met his star athlete until Owens arrived on campus in 1933.

Actually, while Riley was somewhat like a surrogate father to Jesse, Snyder was more of a surrogate brother—an older, more world-wise brother. Snyder was a lot closer to Jesse's age, too. Jesse turned twenty years old in 1933, the autumn that he entered Ohio State; Snyder was just thirty-seven.

Snyder, who had been a track star himself for the Ohio State Buckeyes, had already established himself as a respected and innovative track coach. Immediately he saw the same kind of potential in Jesse that Riley had seen. In 1935, Jesse would break Snyder's own school record for points scored in a single season. "Owens came to Ohio State a great athlete," Snyder once said. "It has been my job to keep him one."

Record-Setting Performance

During Jesse's time, and for several decades afterward, National Collegiate Athletic Association (NCAA) rules didn't allow athletes to compete at the **varsity** level during their freshman years. So Jesse had to be content with participating in freshman meets, invitational meets that were not part of school competitions, and special exhibitions staged by Coach Snyder.

Jesse soon earned a nickname for his speed: "the Buckeye Bullet." His reputation had grown so much that sometimes when he was on the track for an exhibition race or a long-jump competition, he would overshadow Ohio State's varsity meets—spectators would pay more attention to his events than to those of the older, more experienced competitors.

Late in his freshman year, Jesse had a big day at a freshman meet in Columbus. He not only won all three of his events, but he also set new Big Ten freshman records in each of them: 9.6 seconds for the 100-yard dash; 21 seconds for the 220-yard dash; and 24 feet 10 inches for the long jump. (The Big Ten is a college sports conference, made up of schools in the upper

All Distances Are Not Equal

Sometimes Jesse Owens and his fellow competitors ran distances measured off in yards, and sometimes in meters. In high-school and college competitions in the United States, events in Jesse's time were run in yards. In international competition, they were run in meters.

The 100-yard dash was roughly equivalent to the 100 meters, the 220-yard dash to the 200 meters, and so on. A meter, however, is a little longer than a yard. It takes just about 1.09 yards to make a meter; 100 meters, then, is the same as about 109 yards. Looking at it the other way, 100 yards equals only 91.44 meters. So times for the 100-meter dash are always a little better than times for the 100-yard dash.

Today, meters are almost universally used in track-and-field competition.

Midwest and East. Several of those schools first agreed to form a partnership in 1896, with others invited to join over the years. Today, the Big Ten actually has eleven schools: Penn State became the eleventh member in 1990.)

That was an amazing effort, but Owens was just getting warmed up. The following spring, while competing for Ohio State in the Big Ten Championships in Ann Arbor, Michigan, on May 25, 1935, Jesse had what is usually considered the greatest single-day performance in the history of track and field.

In forty-five minutes at Ferry Field—which would have been Jesse's home track had he attended Michigan—the Buckeye

Owens shows off his sprinting form in this c. 1935 photograph at Ohio State. He was an immediate sensation after enrolling at the university in 1933, setting several records.

Bullet broke three world records and equaled another. That was an incredible feat—no one had even established two new world records on the same day before.

Jesse had no trouble winning each of the four events he entered in Ann Arbor: the 100-yard dash, the long jump, the 220-yard dash, and the 220-yard hurdles.

"You saw those things, but it was hard to believe they were happening," remembered former University of Illinois Coach Bob Wright, who in 1935 was a student competing for the school. "After the long jump, people looked at each other and said, 'It can't be.' But you had just seen it."

In a Zone

Jesse's day began in the 100-yard dash. Anyone who did not know who the Buckeye Bullet was might not have been impressed at first. "I really did get a bad start," he said after the race. In the early portion of the race, there was no distance between Jesse and the other competitors. Quickly, though, Jesse shifted into another gear, leaving the pack of elite Big Ten runners behind.

Jesse won easily, finishing in 9.4 seconds to equal the world record. Frank Wykoff, who eventually would run on the same sprint-relay team as Jesse in the 1936 Olympics, originally had set that mark in Chicago in June 1930. Jesse had first tied that standard in 1933. Actually, in Ann Arbor, two of the three official timers had clocked Jesse at 9.3 seconds. But only the slowest time was allowed, which dropped him to 9.4.

After that, Jesse hurried over to the long-jump competition. It was held in the middle of the football field, where track officials had constructed a makeshift pit. Owens was the center of attention. "The whole attention of the crowd was on Jesse, and he asked the broad-jump official to put a white handkerchief out twenty-six feet two inches from the board," Larry Snyder said.

That was the world record, which had been set in 1931 by a Japanese star named Chuhei Nambu. Jesse wanted something to shoot for.

With every eye in the stands on him, Jesse sailed past the handkerchief on his first jump. Jesse not only broke the world record, but he did it by 6¼ inches. That may not sound like much, but it is unheard of in track and field. Most marks are improved upon by the slimmest of margins.

Initially, the fans weren't sure they could believe what they had just witnessed. "The 12,000 spectators were alternately stunned into silence and then moved to tremendous applause when the Buckeye ace staged his almost unbelievable show," one Cleveland newspaper reported.

Owens had eyed the world record in the long jump all season. He hopped up and down in excitement when it was clear that he had surpassed the old mark, even though track officials took several minutes before announcing it to the crowd. They measured and re-measured to make sure they got it right.

Jesse couldn't wait for the official announcement, though. He broke into a wide smile as David Albritton and other teammates came over to congratulate him, then he dusted the sand from his white Ohio State running shorts and hurried over to the start of the 220-yard dash. There would be time later to reflect on his record jump. Ten minutes after the long jump, the starter's gun went off for the 220. Jesse needed only 20.3 seconds to cross the finish line—a remarkable three-tenths of a second better than the previous world record—and win that event.

Broad Jump or Long Jump?

When Coach Snyder refers to the "broad jump," he's talking about the long jump. In fact, most history books and Olympic records books note Jesse Owens's accomplishments in the "broad jump."

Long jump and broad jump are simply different names for the same event. "Broad jump" was more common in Jesse's time; "long jump" is more common now.

Jesse was the greatest long jumper of his generation. The current world-record holder in the long jump (as of 2009) is Mike Powell. He leaped 8.95 meters—or 29.36 feet—in Tokyo in 1991.

Jesse wasn't just a sprinter at Ohio State. He also was one of the greatest long jumpers in college track-and-field history.

Jesse leaves the rest of the runners far behind en route to setting a world record in the 220-yard dash in Ann Arbor, Michigan, in 1935.

Jesse was in a zone. Everything he had trained for had come together on this perfect day. Now there was only one event left: the 220-yard hurdles. The hurdles were not Jesse's strongest event, and he did not particularly enjoy competing in them. But he won that race, too. That wasn't a big surprise. By now, track fans expected Jesse to win just about any event that he entered. His time, though, sent the crowd into another frenzy: 22.6 seconds, another world record.

Forty-five minutes. Four events. Four victories. Three world records shattered and another equaled. It was a single-day performance never before seen in track-and-field competition—and not seen since.

Jesse's Records

Here are the records Jesse broke (or tied) that day in Ann Arbor in 1935. His mark in the long jump is particularly noteworthy because it stood for a remarkable twenty-five years. His jump of 8.13 meters was not bettered until the United States' Ralph Boston leaped 8.21 meters in 1960.

Event	Previous Record	Jesse's Mark
100-Yard Dash	9.4 seconds	9.4 seconds (tied mark)
Long Jump	7.98 meters	8.13 meters
220-Yard Dash	20.6 seconds	20.3 seconds
220-Yard Hurdles	23.0 seconds	22.6 seconds

Ralph Boston, shown here competing in the 1960 Olympic Games in Rome, Italy, broke the world record in the long jump a quarter century after Owens set the mark in 1935.

Red Simmons, who worked at the meet, told a Columbus sportswriter seventy years after the fact: "Considering the equipment he used and the surface he ran on, I think it was the greatest performance any athlete will ever do in any sport." Simmons meant that Jesse didn't have the advantages of modern track surfaces and runners' apparel, which are designed to maximize speed and performance.

The magnitude of Jesse's day even overwhelmed Mr. Riley. When he came out of the stands to congratulate his star pupil, he couldn't find the right words. He simply put his head on Jesse's shoulder and started to cry.

A Bad Fall

Ironically, Jesse's record-setting day at Ann Arbor might never had happened if he had not injured his back the week before the meet. By that time, he had joined a **fraternity** at Ohio State. He and some of his fraternity brothers had been roughhousing, and Jesse fell down some stairs. The night before the Big Ten Championships, Jesse was still in great pain.

Coach Riley could tell something was wrong the first time that he saw Jesse the day of the meet. Riley had made the 140-mile trip in his old Model T to watch Jesse run. But Jesse didn't even warm up before the 100-yard dash. Coach Riley knew his former pupil well enough: something was wrong.

Coach Snyder gave Jesse the okay—told him, actually—to sit out the meet. The conference championships were a big deal, but there would be even bigger competitions coming up soon—like the Olympic Games. The

Coach Riley could tell something was wrong the first time that he saw Jesse the day of the meet.

Olympic Trials were barely more than one year away. Already, the buzz about Jesse was growing. There was no need to risk further injury, and maybe take away America's best hope in the Games.

But Jesse never wanted to be idle. And he certainly didn't want to let down his teammates. Without him, they had no chance at making a run at the Big Ten title. And then he remembered something that Riley had told him several years earlier: sometimes injuries can help you maintain focus. Riley was convinced that if an injury wasn't serious enough to keep an athlete from competing, it forced him or her to keep it from becoming a distraction by focusing extra hard on the task at hand.

So Jesse convinced Snyder to let him have a go at the 100, then to see how he felt. "And when that starter said, 'Get set,' all Jesse's pains vanished," Snyder said. Owens was so focused on the competition that he forgot about the hurt.

The pains returned only when the meet was over and Jesse returned to the Ohio State campus. "And then they had to carry me upstairs," Jesse said.

CHAPTER 6

Olympic Dreams

All I could think about was winning one or two of those gold medals.

Jesse's big day in Ann Arbor set in motion a flurry of events. He was now without question America's premier track-and-field athlete. And every **promoter** wanted America's premier track-and-field athlete at his meet. Every fan wanted to shake his hand. Every newspaper sportswriter wanted to interview him.

Thus, 1935 turned out to be a whirlwind year for Jesse. At first, that was just fine with him. Jesse never wanted to be idle. He wasn't one for sitting still. That may explain in part his love of running. "Being in motion was always what made me tick," Jesse said.

Jesse never wanted to be idle. He wasn't one for sitting still. That may explain in part his love of running.

Jesse was a man constantly in motion—on or off the track. Even after a big meet, when his teammates and coach were ready for some rest, Jesse was ready to hit the town. He could spend a whole night dancing. Coach Snyder knew Jesse thrived on the action. "Put on your [fancy clothes] and get going," he told Jesse one night after a big race. That was how Jesse relaxed, and Coach Snyder knew it was good for his star athlete.

Jesse is pictured at the start of the 60-yard dash at the Millrose Games in New York City's Madison Square Garden in 1935. Though some of the other runners appear to be off to better starts, Jesse still won the race.

More Star Performances

Jesse carried the Buckeyes' Big Ten Championships hopes that season. It was almost an afterthought considering his record-shattering day, but Ohio State equaled its highest finish thus far by coming in second at the Big Ten Championships. Jesse accounted for 40 of the Buckeyes' 43.5 points. All by himself, he outscored every other team except for champion Michigan, which won the meet with 48 points.

A little more than two weeks after the Big Ten Championships in May, Ohio State's track team boarded a train headed for an important meet in Los Angeles, California. Jesse won several events in that meet against the powerful University of Southern California (USC) track team. The next week, he won the 100- and 220-yard dashes, the 220-yard low hurdles, and the long jump—the same four events he took at the Big Ten Championships—at the NCAA championships in Berkeley, California.

Jesse breaks the tape to win the 220-yard dash in a meet against Southern California in the Los Angeles Memorial Coliseum in 1935. He won all four events that he entered in the meet.

USC won that meet to begin a string of nine consecutive national titles, but Ohio State was second. Jesse's four victories accounted for 40 of the Buckeyes' 40.2 points. By himself, Jesse Owens was the second-best college track *team* in the country.

Trouble with Ruth

The events of 1935 proved to be too much even for Jesse, though. For one thing, his relationship with Ruth was rocky. When the team got to Los Angeles, Jesse was the main attraction. Not only did the sportswriters of the area want to meet him, but so did entertainers, movie stars, and **socialites**. One of the socialites was a woman named Quincella Nickerson, with whom Jesse spent several evenings out on the town.

Jesse didn't realize that he had become such a big star that if he went out on the town, photographers were sure to follow. Nor did he realize that the pictures they took would look suspicious when Ruth saw them printed in the Cleveland newspapers. To her, they would look as if he and Quincella were on a date. At first, Ruth, understandably, had her feelings hurt. She wrote an angry letter to Jesse that arrived in California just before the track team headed back to Ohio. After stopping in Lincoln, Nebraska, for a track meet in which Jesse did not do well—his mind surely was on the fractured relationship with Ruth—the team went back to Columbus. Jesse, though, took a different train to Cleveland, where he went straight to Ruth's house. She and Jesse patched things up, and the two decided

> *When the team got to Los Angeles, Jesse was the main attraction. Not only did the sportswriters of the area want to meet him, but so did entertainers, movie stars, and socialites.*

Back from California, Jesse marries Ruth in the living room of the Solomon family home on July 5, 1935. Ernest Hall is the presiding minister.

to get married right away. They called a minister, and they were married in the living room of Ruth's family's house.

Obstacles on the Path

It looked as if nothing could stop Jesse, America's premier track-and-field athlete, all the way to the Olympics in Berlin, Germany. But his path to the Games was not without obstacles.

One of those obstacles was Eulace Peacock, a runner who threatened Jesse's superiority in the sprints. Like Owens, Peacock had been born in Alabama, but he'd been raised in the North—

his family had moved to New Jersey when he was a youngster. Peacock, who went to Temple University in Philadelphia, Pennsylvania, equaled the world record in the 100-meter dash when he ran a race in 10.3 seconds in Oslo, Norway, in 1934.

Either because Jesse's mind was distracted by the whirlwind year, or because his body was overworked, his performance on the track started to suffer. By the end of his active year in 1935, Jesse was worn down—emotionally and physically. Things were happening "so fast that I could hardly keep up with them," he recalled many years later.

One week after the 1935 NCAA championships, Peacock beat Owens in both the 100-yard dash and the long jump in an Amateur Athletic Union (AAU) meet in Nebraska. It was no fluke. Several days later, Peacock beat Jesse in the 100 again in a meet in Ontario, Canada. Then he did it in New York. "I can't help but think that Owens is pretty much burned out," Charles Paddock, Jesse's Olympic inspiration, told the *Los Angeles Times*. Paddock believed that Owens should give up on the 100 for the Olympics and concentrate on the 220. He felt that Jesse was too slow at the start,

"I can't help but think that Owens is pretty much burned out," . . .

and that he didn't have enough time to make up ground in the shorter race. Besides, Peacock was now rapidly becoming the favorite to take home the gold in the 100 meters at the Olympics.

But Jesse's troubles with his starts—and with beating Peacock—paled in comparison to his troubles with the AAU. In August 1935, that organization held a hearing to determine if Jesse violated his amateur status—and in turn, his eligibility to compete in the Olympic Games—by being paid for his work as a **page** in the Ohio legislature. Under the much stricter amateur

This is a photograph of the Ohio State Capitol Building in Columbus as it appeared in 1929. Several years later, Jesse began working as a page in the state legislature.

rules of the time, athletes could not make any money when their sport was in season. Plus, even though Jesse's job there was like those that many athletes had in those days—the demands on his time were minimal—the AAU questioned it because Jesse was paid even when the legislature was not in session.

For three weeks, Jesse had to hold his breath waiting for the AAU to rule on his status in 1936. In the end, the AAU ruled in his favor, and he was still eligible for the Olympics.

Headed for Berlin

With his amateur status secured, Jesse put the busy year of 1935 behind him. With the help of Coach Snyder, he began training in earnest for his ultimate goal: the Olympic Games.

Amateur Rules

Today, National Basketball Association (NBA) players and other professional athletes routinely compete in the Olympic Games.

In Jesse Owen's time, however, the Games were strictly an amateur event. Athletes were not allowed to earn money to play sports. In 1913, the legendary Jim Thorpe was stripped of the two gold medals that he won in track and field at the 1912 Olympics in Stockholm, Sweden, after officials discovered that he had been paid a little money to play baseball for a semipro team in North Carolina in 1909 and 1910. (The medals weren't returned to Thorpe's family until 1983, thirty years after his death.)

Soon, though, some countries, especially in the **Communist** bloc of Eastern Europe, began making a mockery of amateur status. Countries such as the Soviet Union and East Germany essentially paid athletes to train on a full-time basis while calling them students or soldiers.

In the United States, the Amateur Sports Act of 1978 relaxed some of the stricter amateur rules. By the 1990s, professionals began competing in the Olympics.

First, after having to sit out the indoor track season that winter because of his poor grades, Jesse worked hard to get himself academically eligible to compete at Ohio State. While that would not have changed his Olympic status, it did have a big bearing on his chances of making the United States team. If Jesse wasn't eligible, he couldn't use Ohio State's facilities to train every day, and he couldn't compete against the top-flight competition that the Buckeyes faced. If he was forced to work out on his own, he might very well have lost the edge that a great athlete needs to reach his potential.

Studying was hard work for Jesse, but he improved his grades enough that he was eligible for the 1936 spring outdoor season at Ohio State. He worked hard on improving his starts, too. His name soon was back in the winner's column.

At the Penn Relays—one of the biggest and most important track-and-field meets in the world outside of the Olympic Games—in April, Jesse won the 100 meters (in a meet-record time) and the long jump. Meanwhile, Peacock injured his hamstring in the same meet.

Peacock and Owens had become friends off the track even though they were big foes on it. Once, in an exhibition race in Cleveland in 1936, Jesse beat Peacock when Eulace stumbled and fell at the start. That disappointed the fans, who wanted to see two of the top sprinters in the world go at it, and it disappointed Jesse, who wanted to beat his opponents at their best. So when the short 50-yard race was over, Jesse had a solution. "Let's do it again," he told Eulace. The crowd roared its approval, not only because they would get another chance to see the two sprinters in action, but also because of Jesse's amazing gesture of sportsmanship. Peacock won the restart, but Jesse won over a lot of fans that day.

> *The crowd roared its approval, not only because they would get another chance to see the two sprinters in action, but also because of Jesse's amazing gesture of sportsmanship.*

Jesse, then, took no pleasure in seeing his friend injured at the Penn Relays. He knew that an injury of that sort only four

Jesse greets Temple University star Eulace Peacock at a meet in Lincoln, Nebraska, in 1935. Although they were rivals on the track, Owens and Peacock became good friends.

months before the Olympics was a huge setback, and he was right. Although Olympic officials bent the rules to allow Peacock to make it to the Olympic Trials Finals, he never recovered sufficiently in time to make the 1936 Olympic team.

In May 1936, nearly a full calendar year after Jesse equaled the world record in the 100-yard dash in Ann Arbor, he broke the mark in Ohio State's meet against the University of Wisconsin. In that meet in Madison, Wisconsin, he ran 100 yards in 9.3 seconds. Then came the Big Ten Championships. Jesse easily repeated as the champ in all four of his events again.

After that, the next big test came in regional qualifying for the Olympics in Chicago in June. Four years earlier, Jesse had

Jesse wins the 200-meter final at the United States Olympic Trials at Randall's Island, New York, in 1936. In second place is Mack Robinson (with a "P" on his jersey for Pasadena City College), the brother of baseball pioneer Jackie Robinson.

been in awe of the immense talent he encountered. This time, it was the other competitors who were in awe of him. He easily qualified for the next step in Princeton, New Jersey, in July, and from there for the Olympic Trials Finals at Randall's Island, New York, on July 11 and 12.

At Randall's Island, Jesse won both the 100-meter and 200-meter dashes, as well as the long jump. Jesse's Olympic dream had come true. He officially was a member of the United States team for the 1936 Games. In a few days, he would be on a ship headed for Germany. The next task was winning a gold medal. "While I was going over on the boat, all I could think about was winning one or two of those gold medals," he said.

One goal met, one more to go.

Jesse's Chief Olympic Rivals

It was a foregone conclusion that the winner of the men's 100 meters at the 1936 Olympics in Berlin would be from the United States. After all, the top sprinters in the world were all American, including Jesse Owens.

It was far from certain, however, whether Owens would win the gold medal. Eulace Peacock already had proved to be a formidable rival, and was given a chance to make the Olympic team all the way up to the Trials Finals at Randall's Island in July. With Peacock still slowed by his injured hamstring, Ralph Metcalfe and Frank Wykoff were the most likely candidates to win gold in the 100 at Berlin.

Metcalfe had won two sprint medals in the 1932 Olympics in Los Angeles, taking home a silver medal in the 100 meters and a bronze in the 200. He went to college at Marquette University, where he won NCAA championships at both 100 yards and 220 yards for three consecutive years beginning in 1932.

At twenty-six years old in 1936, Wykoff may have been past his prime, but he was still a worthy and experienced contender who was competing in the Olympics for the third time. In all three Games (1928, 1932, and 1936), the University of Southern California star helped the United States win a gold medal in the 4 × 100 meter relay in world-record time.

Frank Wykoff (third from right) was one of Jesse's chief competitors for gold at the 1936 Olympics. Wykoff, shown here as a high school sensation in 1928, was a veteran of the previous two Olympic Games.

CHAPTER 7

The Nazi Olympics

[The Olympics represented a] great opportunity to strike a blow at Hitler.

> —The National Association for the Advancement of Colored People (NAACP)

Among the athletes to qualify for the United States Olympic Team in 1936 were nineteen African Americans. Of those, thirteen—including Jesse Owens, of course—competed in track and field. One of the others was high jumper David Albritton, who was Jesse's longtime friend. Another was Mack Robinson, a sprinter from the Los Angeles area. Robinson was the older brother of Jackie Robinson, the man who would break major-league baseball's color barrier. Jackie became the first black man

to play on a major-league team when he joined the Brooklyn Dodgers in 1947.

The African Americans on the United States track team did not have to face as many taunts and

Jackie Robinson was the man who broke Major League Baseball's color barrier in 1947. Jackie's older brother, Mack, was a member of the United States' Olympic track team in 1936.

insults from fellow competitors as Jackie Robinson would have to endure eleven years later. After all, they weren't the first African American competitors in their sport. And none of them had to go it alone like Jackie did. But their role was difficult nonetheless. They were traveling to a country that was openly hostile to minorities, a country whose political leaders promoted its citizens as intellectually, morally, and athletically superior to those who didn't look the same as they did.

The International Olympic Committee (IOC) had originally awarded the 1936 Games to Germany in 1931, before Chancellor Adolf Hitler and his National Socialist German Workers Party— the Nazi Party—had come to power. Hitler took control in 1933; soon afterward, some nations began having reservations about sending their athletes to the 1936 Games. Although Hitler had not yet made military maneuvers that resulted in the start of World War II in 1939, his political views were known. Hitler believed that **Aryans** were superior to all other people, and he treated non-Aryans as less-than-human. This included African Americans and others who were visible minorities because of the color of their skin, as well as Jewish people, and anyone else who didn't fit the German ideal.

Owens and his teammates were intensely aware of Hitler's spite for them. "We were everything Hitler hated," Jesse once wrote. "Other people—the Jews, Poles, and others Hitler hungered to have abjectly kneeling at his feet—at least didn't have their beliefs written on their very skins. But, in particular, Hitler hated my skin."

For a while after Hitler became chancellor in 1933, nations turned a blind eye to such hatred. But by 1936, the world was beginning to see the potential for the horrors that were to come later in Hitler's **regime**. For instance, the infamous Nuremberg

Atmosphere of Hate

Anti-Semitism rapidly became a way of life in Germany. Anti-Semitism means discriminating against people simply because they are Jewish. German leader Adolf Hitler began removing Jewish people from any positions of influence. Jews could not hold any political office. They could not work in civil-service jobs or teach at universities. They could not marry non-Jews. Anti-Jewish signs and slogans were posted all over Germany, and Jewish storefronts were routinely vandalized.

Hitler didn't just dislike Jewish people. It went far beyond that. He considered them inferior to non-Jewish Germans. Indeed, he considered any non-Aryans to be inferior. Although privately he acknowledged that Jesse Owens and his dark-skinned teammates on the United States squad would dominate the track-and-field portion of the Olympics, publicly he ridiculed them.

It all added up to an atmosphere of hate and intolerance that led to the horror of the Holocaust— the killing of more than 6 million Jewish people, and others, during World War II.

The sign in this 1935 photograph reads JEWS NOT WANTED IN THIS PLACE! Such messages were prevalent in Germany before and after the 1936 Olympics—but were not often seen during the Games.

Nazis celebrate Nazi Party Day in Nuremberg, Germany, in 1934. The Nazi Party eventually would become infamous for horrors inflicted upon Jews and other non-Aryans.

Laws were passed in Germany in September of 1935. The Nuremberg Laws made Jews noncitizens and took away any rights and protections they had.

Hitler had publicly made disapproving remarks about the Olympics, but his advisors convinced him that hosting the Games would be a good **propaganda** tool. He could use the Games to spread his ideas about the superiority of the Aryan race. Some political leaders and Olympic personnel outside of Germany called for the Games to be moved. The Olympics could not be moved, though. The challenge of putting on the Games is so great that they have to be awarded many years in advance.

Besides, the International Olympic Committee has always believed that the Games should be separate from politics. Plus, when Avery Brundage, the head of the United States Olympic Committee, visited Germany in the summer of 1934, he had been carefully escorted around so that many of the horrible things going on in that country were hidden from him. There wasn't an anti-Jewish sign in sight, and the Jews paraded before Brundage had no complaints. So the 1936 Games went on in Germany as planned.

The next idea proposed was to **boycott** the 1936 Games. That meant certain nations not sending their athletes to Germany for the Games. The Olympic boycott movement was strongest in the United States, where Jesse Owens and the other American Olympians were thrust into a political debate.

Stuck in the Middle

American athletes such as Jesse Owens found themselves in the midst of the fight over whether it was appropriate to hold the Olympics in a political climate such as Germany's in the 1930s.

One side of the debate called for boycotting the Olympics because any country that was noninclusive and treated certain people as less-than-human should not be rewarded with the Games.

The other side of the debate called for sending athletes, particularly African American athletes, to the Games in Germany. The argument on this side of the debate was that the athletes would win in Berlin, which would prove the notion of Aryan superiority wrong.

The National Association for the Advancement of Colored People (**NAACP**) reflected these conflicting views. The NAACP publicly called for a boycott, but at the same time the

1980 Olympic Boycott

While a boycott of the 1936 Olympics never happened, the United States did organize a boycott more than four decades later to protest the Soviet Union's 1979 invasion of Afghanistan.

The 1980 Summer Games were held in Moscow in the Soviet Union. President Jimmy Carter vowed that the United States would not participate in the Games if Soviet troops did not withdraw from Afghanistan by February 20, 1980. The troops did not withdraw, and the United States followed through on its threat. A number of other large countries, such as Japan, West Germany, and China, joined in the boycott.

In retaliation for the United States' boycott of the Moscow Games, the Soviet Union did not send any of its athletes to the 1984 Olympics in Los Angeles, California.

Jimmy Carter was the thirty-ninth president of the United States (January 1977–January 1981). He ordered the United States boycott of the 1980 Olympic Games in Moscow.

organization sensed that the Games also represented a "great opportunity to strike a blow at Hitler."

In December of 1935, Walter White, the leader of the NAACP, drafted a letter to Jesse. In the two-page letter, White wrote that "it was with deep regret that I read in the New York press today a statement attributed to [you] saying that you would participate in the 1936 Olympic Games even if they are held in Germany under the Hitler regime."

White acknowledged that it would take a tremendous sacrifice for Owens to give up his Olympic dream. However, he also believed that African Americans on the U.S. team were impressive enough to win, which would challenge Hitler's Aryan ideal. If black athletes competed—and won—at the Games, it could help to diminish racial bigotry.

In other words, White was as ambivalent about the boycott as a lot of people in the United States. There were pros and cons on both sides. In fact, White was so conflicted that he never sent off the letter to Owens.

Interestingly, no one thought that Jesse and his teammates might go over to Germany and potentially *lose*. The American track stars clearly were the best in the world, and they fully expected to win at the Games.

Jesse fully expected to win, too, and he wanted no part of the boycott. Like most athletes, his single-minded pursuit was Olympic glory. The political issues were for the politicians. Besides, where Owens lived, African Americans often couldn't eat at the same restaurants, stay at the same hotels, or sit in the same seats on a bus as white Americans. Many critics

The American track stars clearly were the best in the world, and they fully expected to win at the Games.

of the boycott movement in the United States reasoned that it would be hypocritical to hold Germany responsible for its prejudices when there still was so much prejudice in Owens's own country.

Propaganda Triumph

Unlike the way it would be in 1947 for Jackie Robinson, who was one black face in an otherwise all-white baseball society, the African Americans on the United States Olympic Team at least had one another to lean on. In fact, sprinter Ralph Metcalfe called a meeting of all the African American track-and-field athletes on the boat trip over to Berlin. He counseled that they

Several African Americans on the 1936 U.S. Olympic Team posed for this picture. Ralph Metcalfe, whom Jesse called a calming influence, is the third athlete from the right (standing in white jacket and tie). Jesse's good friend David Albritton is at the far left.

Jesse exhibits his hurdling form before a crowd of passengers on the SS *Manhattan* on the way to Berlin in July 1936.

not get caught up in politics in Berlin, that they focus on what they were there for. "That led to our success," Jesse said. "He calmed our fears." Even still, when the members of the team disembarked from the boat that carried them to Europe, they were wary of the greeting they would get from their hosts.

But the reception surprised them. Even if Hitler and the German government were openly disdainful of African Americans, the German people certainly were not. They greeted the American team—especially Owens—with enthusiasm. Jesse was besieged by autograph seekers and people wanting to take his photograph. If anything, the outpouring of affection was too much. Jesse needed time to train. He needed space to get his track legs back after more than a week at sea.

German fans enthusiastically welcomed the United States team to the 1936 Olympics. In this photo, they surround Owens for autographs on the day of the Opening Ceremonies.

Later, once the Games started, the crowds at the Olympic Stadium in Berlin would chant Jesse's name in unison.

The Games themselves were a spectacular display of pageantry, including the first Olympic Torch Relay. Historian David Clay Large called it the Nazis' "first big international show." Indeed, the Germans put on a performance for the world, hiding the growing wickedness going on behind the scenes.

Most historians call the 1936 Games a propaganda triumph for the Nazis because Germany was cast in the best possible light. By almost any standard, the Games were considered a rousing success, with the world treated to views of German pomp and goodwill. Author Jeremy Schaap, however, points out that the 1936 Olympics were intended not to promote the

Olympic Torch Relay

The Olympic Torch Relay is a familiar sight to fans of the Games: the Olympic flame is carried by a succession of torchbearers from Olympia, Greece, to whichever city is the host of that year's Summer or Winter Games. At the Olympic Stadium, the torch lights a flame to culminate the Opening Ceremonies, and the Games are officially open.

While the origins of the Olympic flame come from ancient Greece—in Greek mythology, Prometheus stole fire from the mighty god Zeus and gave it to mortals—the Olympic Torch Relay is a thoroughly modern event. The tradition began at the 1936 Olympics in Berlin.

Beginning at Olympia on July 20, the torch was carried across Europe by more than 3,000 runners, each of whom covered just about a kilometer (0.62 miles) of the route. A man named Fritz Schilgen, who was chosen for his Aryan looks and graceful running style, carried the torch on its final leg into the Olympic Stadium.

This is the lighting of the Olympic Torch at the opening of the 1936 Games.

Like just about everything else concerning the 1936 Games, the Olympic Torch Relay was a propaganda tool of the Nazis. Historian David Clay Large called it "an advertisement for the new Germany across southeastern and central Europe." Hitler and his followers imagined that ancient Greece was the predecessor to their modern Germany—and to their belief in Aryan supremacy. The torch relay was a way to symbolically bridge that gap.

Nazis' political views, "but to hide their agenda under a cloak of hospitality."

Athletes at the 1936 Games were treated remarkably well by their hosts. Jesse and the other male athletes were housed in a modern-style Olympic Village about fifteen miles west of Berlin (The female athletes were housed in a separate dormitory closer to the stadium.) The village had everything the athletes needed: shops, a library, training facilities—even a cinema. No matter which nation an athlete was from, he could get the kind of food that he was accustomed to at home.

Jesse was happy with the accommodations. Now all that was left was to win gold.

The above photograph shows the room in which Jesse Owens stayed in the Olympic Village near Berlin in 1936. After the Olympics, these rooms were used as military barracks until the early 1990s.

CHAPTER 8

The Games Begin

All these years of hard work—I'm going to make sure they were worthwhile.

The Opening Ceremonies of the 1936 Games were held on Saturday, August 1. More than 110,000 fans crammed into Olympic Stadium to watch the athletes from each participating country march around the track. Back home, Ruth's and Jesse's parents anxiously huddled near the radio waiting for word about Jesse. Coach Snyder made the trip to Berlin with Jesse, although only as his personal coach and not as an official member of the United States staff.

One member of each country's Olympic team led the rest of the squad into the stadium by carrying its national flag. The biggest cheers, of course, were for the German team, whose members displayed the infamous "Heil Hitler" salute as they walked past the German chancellor's box in the stands.

The Germans put on an incredible show with fireworks,

This artwork is from a poster of the Olympic Games in Berlin in 1936.

Flag Tradition

During the Opening Ceremonies of the 1936 Games, the United States team was the last national group before the host Germans to parade into the Olympic Stadium. Unlike each of the nations to precede it, however, the United States did not bow its flag in respect as it passed the Honor Loge in which German Chancellor Adolf Hitler sat.

This was not a political statement directed at Hitler or the Nazi Party, however. Instead, it is a tradition that began in 1908 at the Olympic Games—and continues to this day. In London in 1908, American flag carrier Ralph Rose refused to dip the flag as the United States team passed the royal box. "This flag dips to no earthly king," American captain Martin Sheridan reportedly said.

Flag bearer Lopez Lomong leads the United States team at the Olympic Games in Beijing, China, in 2008. It is a tradition that the American flag "dips to no earthly king."

music, and speeches—the kind of Opening Ceremonies that have now become expected at the Games. Overhead, the *Hindenburg* flew past. It was, one writer said, a "pageant such as the modern world seldom has witnessed."

After all the athletes were in, German runner Fritz Schilgen entered the stadium with the Olympic flame. Schilgen was blond and blue-eyed—the perfect representation of Hitler's Aryan ideal. Schilgen climbed the steps at the east end of the stadium and lit the torch. "I announce as open the games of Berlin," Hitler said in German, and the Games had officially begun.

Jesse took in all the pageantry. He couldn't wait to get started. "All these years of hard work—I'm going to make sure they were worthwhile," he confided to a reporter.

It wasn't long before Jesse got his chance to compete. The track-and-field events began in the same stadium on August 2. The morning of the first day of competition included the qualifying races in the 100-meter dash; the afternoon included the semifinal. The final was the next afternoon.

Because sixty-eight runners were trying to qualify for only six spots in the 100-meter final, Jesse had to survive the first round of preliminary races and then the semifinal round just for a chance at the gold medal. (He did not necessarily have to win the qualifying races, but he had to post a time good enough to make it to the final.) He was a little nervous. Jesse had dreamed of competing in the Olympics ever since that day at Fairmount Junior High when he met Charles Paddock. But now he wanted more than that. He wanted to win a gold medal. He didn't want, as he later put it, for one mistake to ruin those eight years of training.

As it turned out, there was nothing to worry about. After watching eleven other heats, or qualifying races, it was Jesse's

The *Hindenburg*

Spectators waiting for the arrival of Adolf Hitler and the Opening Ceremonies of the 1936 Olympic Games could look up and admire the sight of the giant blimp *Hindenburg* flying overhead, an Olympic banner in tow.

The *Hindenburg* was the largest airship ever to fly. It was 803.8 feet in length and 135.1 feet in diameter. Although it had been in use only since March 1936, it had been back and forth across the Atlantic Ocean several times. In June of that year, the *Hindenburg* carried boxer Max Schmeling back to a hero's welcome in Frankfurt, Germany, after his victory over American Joe Louis in a heavyweight title fight in New York. In July, it set a record by making a round-trip across the Atlantic in less than six days.

The *Hindenburg* was fated for disaster, though. Because nonflammable helium was expensive and not readily available, the *Hindenburg* was filled with the flammable gas hydrogen. In May 1937, while attempting to land in Lakehurst, New Jersey, the airship burst into flames. Remarkably, sixty-two of the ninety-seven passengers and crew survived (one person on the ground was killed in addition to thirty-five on the airship).

This drawing depicts the *Hindenburg* as it flew over the Olympic Stadium in Berlin in 1936. Less than one year later, the giant airship burst into flames while attempting to land in New Jersey.

Jesse participated in the last of the opening qualifying races for the 100 meters in Berlin. He's shown here easily outrunning the others in that race to move on to the quarterfinals.

turn. He got in position on the track, and at the sound of the starter's gun, he was off! Jesse left the other runners far behind. At the finish, he was a good 10 feet in front of his nearest pursuer. His time was 10.3 seconds, which equaled not only the Olympic record, but the world record (which he already shared) as well.

In the afternoon quarterfinal, Jesse did even better: 10.2 seconds. The crowd was in awe. "You could hear the chorus of gasps as he left all rivals far behind," famed sportswriter Grantland Rice reported. A tailwind prevented Jesse's time from being recognized as a world record. But that didn't matter. What mattered was that Jesse qualified for the 100-meter semifinals. He had to finish among the top two in the semifinals to reach the finals. That was no problem. Without going all out and risking injury, he ran 10.4 seconds to win his semifinal. Jesse was only one race away from a gold medal.

"The Happiest Day in My Life"

As Jesse settled into his crouch for the start of the final late on Monday afternoon, his eyes focused only on the finish line, 100 meters away. Five world-class sprinters lined up with him, but he wasn't concerned about them. Jesse Owens knew that the only runner he had to worry about was himself. That was something else that he had learned from his mentor. "I'd learned long ago from Charles Riley, the only victory that counts is the one over yourself."

Jesse forgot that lesson the day that he was in awe of the other runners at the 1932 Olympic Trials, but he wasn't going to forget that as he lined up now for the biggest race of his life.

As Jesse settled into his crouch for the start of the final late on Monday afternoon, his eyes focused only on the finish line, 100 meters away.

It had rained the morning of the 100-meter final, but Jesse was spared the inside lane of the cinder track—the starting slot he had drawn—when officials moved everyone over one lane. That was important because the inside lane had been chewed up the most in the soggy conditions.

A lot of runners would have been put off by the weather and the conditions of the track, but Jesse wasn't worried. After all, everyone had to run in the same conditions. Besides, if Jesse was faster than everybody else on a perfect track, he still was faster than everyone else on a track that was less than perfect.

The conditions may have slowed down some of the other runners, but not Jesse. The outcome of the race never was in doubt. Jesse burst into the lead almost from the start and pulled away from the field. Ralph Metcalfe, his fellow American, put on a burst of speed to close the gap at the end and earn the silver

Jesse called the medal ceremony after the 100 meters "the happiest day in my life." He returned atop the medal stand three more times before the Olympics were over, including this time after the long jump.

medal, but the gold was Jesse's. Even in the poor conditions, he equaled the world record again with a time of 10.3 seconds.

Soon afterward, Jesse took his place on the highest level of the awards podium. The United States flag was raised, and "The Star-Spangled Banner" played over the loudspeakers. Jesse was nearly overcome with emotion.

Until his dying day, Owens said this gold-medal ceremony made it "the happiest day in my life."

Snubbed by Hitler?

Jesse did not receive any congratulations from Adolf Hitler after his gold-medal-winning performance in the 100 meters in Berlin—nor did the German chancellor acknowledge any of Owens's subsequent gold medals in the 1936 Games.

This has come to be known as Hitler's "snub" of Owens. It is often offered as both proof of Hitler's hatred of African Americans and a reason for Jesse's inspired performance in the Games.

There have been so many versions of the story over the years, however, that it's hard to know what really happened.

Some details are certain, though. First, while it is unusual for any political leader to receive athletes in his box following an Olympic performance, Hitler did just that after Germans Hans Woellke and Tilly Fleischer won gold medals on the first day of competition on August 2. Woellke, who won the shot put, was the first German man ever to win a gold medal in track and field. Fleischer, who won the javelin, was the first German woman ever to win. Hitler took advantage of the opportunity to shake hands and pose for pictures with his fellow Germans.

The only other gold medal awarded the first day was to the winner of the high-jump competition. American Cornelius Johnson won that competition, beating Jesse's friend David Albritton, by clearing the winning height of 2.03 meters (6 feet 8 inches).

Johnson and Albritton both were African American. Hitler did not receive them in his box, but Hitler was not in the stadium at the conclusion of the high-jump competition. After the first day of competition, Hitler did not congratulate any more winners—including Jesse Owens.

Those are the facts. The rest is purely **conjecture**. Hitler may have left the stadium that first evening because it was apparent that a black American would win the high jump—and he almost certainly did not want to be seen shaking hands with a black American. Or he may have left the stadium because the event ran later than anticipated. (That was the reason given by German

German leader Adolf Hitler (left) is pictured at the 1936 Olympic Games. Standing with him is King Boris of Bulgaria.

officials.) The high jump ended at about 7 o'clock, long after the rest of the day's schedule was done.

After that, the head of the International Olympic Committee asked Hitler that he congratulate either all of the winners or none of them. Hitler chose not to congratulate any more of them. That might have been because it was obvious to the chancellor that congratulating all of the winners was sure to include African Americans, such as Owens, although nobody knows for sure.

In reality, then, Hitler did not snub Owens. "If he snubbed any black American athlete, it was Cornelius Johnson rather than Jesse Owens," wrote William J. Baker, an Owens biographer.

Still, it didn't take long for the story to take on a life of its own. HITLER SNUBS JESSE blared the headline in one Cleveland black newspaper.

Owens himself is guilty of giving life to the myth—and allowing it to grow. After initially dismissing the idea that Hitler snubbed him, he eventually incorporated the story into many of his speeches. Jesse may have come to believe it was true—or he may have believed that it was what his audiences wanted to hear.

CHAPTER 9

More Gold

I had what was most important to me in the world: a chance to rise from Oakville to champion of the entire world.

Adolf Hitler and other German authorities' reaction to Jesse Owens may have been decidedly unfriendly, but the German fans' reaction definitely wasn't. They enthusiastically rooted Owens on from the moment that he first took the track at Olympic Stadium.

The reaction was unexpected, even after seeing the celebrity status that Jesse had at the Olympic Village. "I had braced him for a stony, forbidding silence," Coach Snyder said. Worse still, Snyder had feared insults and taunts from the crowd. He'd warned Jesse to ignore them, and

Jesse is off and running in a 200-meter race at the 1936 Games. Note that he is starting from holes dug into the track, instead of starting blocks as today's runners do.

not allow them to throw off his concentration. But again, Snyder's fears were unfounded.

"Even from a distance, they could see that he was a delightful person, cheerful, easygoing, and generous in victory," writer Duff Hart-Davis noted in *Hitler's Games*.

When Jesse hit the tape crossing the finish line, in the 100-meter final to win his first gold medal, the crowd roared in appreciation. The spectators didn't know yet that Jesse was on the brink of a historic performance. By the time the track-and-field competition was over—all of it took place in the opening week of the 16-day Games—Jesse would become the first American track athlete ever to win four gold medals in one Olympiad.

The Long Jump

Jesse had to work hardest for his gold medal in the long jump. For a while, it looked as if he might not even make it out of the qualifying round, even though he was only a high school student the first time that he soared past the distance (23 feet 5½ inches) necessary to reach the finals.

Owens's chief competition for gold in the long jump was Germany's Luz Long. At 6 feet tall and a chiseled 159 pounds, with blond hair and blue eyes, the 23-year-old Long was everything Hitler promoted in an Aryan athlete. "He sure looks like a Nazi," Coach Snyder said. Long even intimidated Owens a bit. The German had a "perfectly proportioned body," he said.

As it turned out, though, Long was not Owens's enemy, but his friend. Later, Jesse called him "the best friend I ever had. He turned out to be what you might call a messenger from God." Without Long, Jesse might not have won the long jump.

Jesse's custom was to take one run through the long-jump pit without attempting a leap, just to get warmed up and to get

Owens and Luz Long watch fellow competitors in the long jump at the 1936 Games. The German and the American became good friends.

a feel for the track. He followed that custom in Berlin—and up went the official's red flag, indicating a foul. Jesse looked around, stunned. There was no warm-up run allowed, and Jesse didn't know it.

Okay, he thought. No big deal. He still had two more chances to make what was a routine leap for him. On his second try, though, Jesse measured the steps wrong on his approach. His final step crossed the foul line—and up went the red flag again!

Now it was a big deal. He had two fouls, and only one chance left. Jesse might not even make it to the finals. Self-doubt started to creep in. Jesse wasn't used to that. "One cell at a time, panic crept into my body," Jesse recalled many years later.

He looked over at Hitler's box. The Führer (the German word for leader) wasn't there. "His way of saying that Jesse Owens was inferior," Jesse once wrote.

And then, an extraordinary thing happened. Long, Owens's chief rival and the picture of Aryan ideal, calmed Jesse's nerves. He encouraged Jesse to mark off his steps beginning with a spot behind the foul mark. Jesse could take off from 6 to 12 inches behind the line, not have to worry about a foul, and still easily clear the qualifying distance.

Long was right. Jesse leaped more than 25 feet on his final try, and was in the finals. "I didn't know how to thank Luz Long," Jesse wrote many years later. "Because of him, because of his seeing past skin color, nationality, and Hitler's godless

Jesse takes flight in the long jump at the 1936 Games. He nearly failed to make it out of the qualifying round, but in the end won the gold medal.

beliefs, I had what was most important to me in the world: a chance to rise from Oakville to champion of the entire world."

After a quick, 21.1-second sprint to equal an Olympic record in a qualifying round for the 200 meters, Jesse went back to the long-jump pit for the finals, which consisted of two rounds. He and Long staged an amazing duel in which each surpassed the previous Olympic record. On his next-to-last jump, Long jumped 25 feet 10 inches to equal Owens's best. Then Jesse soared 26 feet—he was in the lead! When Long faulted on his final try, Jesse had the gold medal secured. Still, he took his last try and went 5½ inches farther than the last time.

Before the realization of his second gold medal could sink in, someone grabbed Owens by the hand and raised his arm in the air in triumph. It was Long. In a wonderful display of sportsmanship, Long led the crowd in a cheer, chanting Jesse's name.

Owens and Long became very close. They spent hours talking in the Olympic Village. But after the Games, they would never see each other again: Long was killed fighting for the Germans several years later in World War II.

The 200 Meters

Owens's third gold medal came in an easy victory in the 200 meters. Although it was rainy and cold again, and the race was into the wind, Jesse needed only 20.7 seconds to cover the eighth of a mile in the final. That was another world record.

There is a photo of Jesse near the end of his victory in this race. He is coasting to the finish, completely at ease— "such a combination of blazing speed and effortless smoothness," sportswriter Grantland Rice had written about Jesse's style. The photo is a perfect example of the cool efficiency with which Jesse ran. Meanwhile, behind him, all the other competitors are straining, with intense effort apparent on their faces.

Again, Hitler was not on hand to salute Owens's performance—and again there was a ready excuse. "Hitler was driven from his box by a heavy downpour just after Owens flashed across the finish line,"

Owens breezes to victory in the 200 meters at the Olympics. While his competitors' faces strain with exertion, Jesse looks as if he's barely broken a sweat.

In Cleveland, Emma Owens, Jesse's mother, listens intently to the radio for reports from Berlin about her son's performance in the Games.

that evening's Associated Press news report read, "and wasn't among the thousands who thundered acclaim when the American stepped up for the third time to be crowned with a laurel wreath and given his third gold medal."

"Immaterial," Jesse said. Really, what did it matter? The Olympics were only four days old, and Owens already had three gold medals.

The 4 × 100 Meter Relay

In the 4 × 100 meter relay (sometimes called the 400-meter relay or the sprint relay), Jesse was the lead leg in a record-setting effort by the Americans. The United States team of Owens, Ralph Metcalfe, Foy Draper, and Frank Wykoff easily beat the competition to the finish line. Second-place Italy was more than one second behind the winners.

Owens had thought his victory in the 200 meters four days earlier marked the end of a wildly successful Olympic Games for him. He wasn't originally supposed to run in the relay. Marty Glickman and Sam Stoller presumably were set to join Draper and Wykoff in the race. But the relay teams are made up of any qualifying runners. It's a coach's decision—and the night before the relay, U.S. coach Lawson Robertson decided that Owens and Metcalfe would run instead of Glickman and Stoller.

The United States won the gold medal in the 4 × 100 meter relay at the 1936 Games. Owens, who ran the first leg in both the qualifying round and the final, is shown here just after handing off to Ralph Metcalfe for the second leg.

Marty Glickman (1917–2001)

Marty Glickman returned to Olympic Stadium in Berlin in 1985, forty-nine years after he was removed from the United States' 4 × 100 meter relay team on the eve of the competition. He was shocked to feel the anger of the decision well up inside him again.

"I was really amazed at myself, at this feeling of anger," he once said. "Not about the German Nazis—that was a given. But the anger at Avery Brundage and Dean Cromwell for not allowing an eighteen-year-old kid to compete in the Olympic Games just because he was Jewish."

Despite the insult in Berlin, Glickman went on to a successful career in sports. He was an All-American in football at Syracuse University (he was in college at the time of the 1936 Games) and began working at a New York radio station as a sportscaster soon after his graduation.

In 1946, basketball's New York Knickerbockers were founded, and Glickman became the club's radio voice. Over the next forty-six years, he was a mainstay in New York broadcasting. He worked in radio or television for the

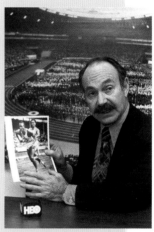

Marty Glickman is pictured in his office in New York in this photograph from 1980. Glickman was a member of the United States Olympic Team in 1936 but did not compete in any event in Berlin.

Knicks, football's New York Giants and New York Jets, baseball's Brooklyn Dodgers (before they moved to California) and New York Yankees, and horse racing's Yonkers Raceway. He was working for the Jets when he retired in 1992. Glickman died at the age of eighty-three in 2001.

But Jesse objected. "Let Marty and Sam run," he insisted in an account backed up by the recollections of several of his teammates. "I've already got three gold medals. I don't need any more."

Glickman and Stoller, both Jewish, hadn't competed in the Olympics at all. It has long been argued that Coach Robertson bowed to pressure not to allow the two Jewish athletes to run. It could have come from either the Germans or from the United States Olympic Committee, headed by Avery Brundage, possibly not wanting to upset the Germans.

"Those boys [Glickman and Stoller] were heartbroken," said Jimmy LuValle, another member of the United States team. "It was quite obvious it had not been done fairly."

No reason was given for the decision, except for an implausible excuse that the Germans had been hiding their best runners, so the United States had to counter with their best runners. Owens would start the relay for the United States team. Again, it was no contest. When Wykoff hit the tape on the anchor leg (the last part of a relay race), the Americans had set another world record: 39.8 seconds. And Jesse Owens had earned his fourth gold medal.

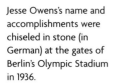

Jesse Owens's name and accomplishments were chiseled in stone (in German) at the gates of Berlin's Olympic Stadium in 1936.

The Gold Standard

In 1936, Jesse Owens became the first American track athlete to win four gold medals in a single Olympics. Here are the results of the finals in those four events:

Men's 100 Meters
1. Jesse Owens, United States   10.3 seconds
2. Ralph Metcalfe, United States   10.4 seconds
3. Tinus Osendarp, Netherlands   10.5 seconds

Men's 200 Meters
1. Jesse Owens, United States   20.7 seconds*
2. Mack Robinson, United States   21.1 seconds
3. Tinus Osendarp, Netherlands   21.3 seconds

Men's 4 × 100 Meter Relay
1. United States   39.8 seconds*
2. Italy   41.1 seconds
3. Germany   41.2 seconds

Men's Long Jump
1. Jesse Owens, United States   8.06 meters
2. Luz Long, Germany   7.87 meters
3. Naoto Tajima, Japan   7.74 meters

*new world record

Jesse, wearing his laurel wreath, displays the three gold medals he won in individual events at the 1936 Games: the 100 meters, 200 meters, and long jump. He also was part of the winning 4 × 100 meter relay team.

CHAPTER 10

After the Games

He was the idol of the country, and a week later he was riding in the back of the bus.

—Marty Glickman

Jesse didn't have long to sit and reflect about his accomplishments at the Games. He was busy packing his bags for a post-Olympic exhibition tour of meets in Europe. The trip had been arranged well in advance of the Olympics as a means of helping to cover the cost of sending the American athletes to the Games. The Amateur Athletic Union had rightly figured that the American track athletes—especially Jesse Owens—would be the stars of the Games and would be a good draw in Europe immediately afterward.

But the Americans were exhausted. There was the long boat trip over from the States . . . the enormous pressure of competing in the Olympics . . . and then the events themselves. Jesse had not only competed in

After his performance at the 1936 Games, Jesse was arguably the most famous athlete in the world. He signs autographs in London in this photo.

the four finals in which he took gold. He had also run several preliminary heats in the 100- and 200-meter races, plus a couple of additional rounds in the long jump.

Coach Snyder was furious when he found out that the AAU planned to run Jesse just two days after the Americans' world-record performance in the relay. The athletes, who were only casually told about the tour on the ship en route to Berlin, weren't much happier. After all, as strict amateurs, they weren't getting paid to perform. Plus, they had already been away from home for several weeks, and many of them had families to consider. Jesse had not only Ruth to provide for, but also his daughter Gloria, who turned four years old the day before Jesse won his fourth gold medal in Berlin. And he still helped out his parents financially whenever he could. He needed to get home and start making some money. Jesse missed them all, too. It had been nearly a month since he had left New York Harbor on the boat for Europe.

Details of the post-Olympics tour were largely kept from the athletes. They weren't sure how long it would be or where they would go. As it turned out, it would take the Americans to cities such as Dresden, Cologne, and Bochum in Germany, as well as London, England, and Stockholm, Sweden. Before the team headed to Cologne, the Associated Press reported, "Jesse Owens will turn professional if there is enough money in it, he announced."

Turning pro meant that Jesse could command money to take part in track meets, regardless of whether he won or

> *Coach Snyder was furious when he found out that the AAU planned to run Jesse just two days after the Americans' world-record performance in the relay.*

not. It meant being able to lend his name to products and advertisements. But it also meant that he would not be eligible to compete in his final season at Ohio State—and he would not be eligible for the Olympic Games in 1940. (As it turned out, those Games never were held because of the onset of World War II.)

There were pros and cons on both sides. Jesse was leaning toward going professional, but in the end, a decision by the AAU left him with no choice. His amateur days were about to end.

The Stockholm Incident

Cramped train quarters, bumpy plane rides, and a hectic schedule combined to make for some lackluster performances on the exhibition tour. Before 35,000 fans in Cologne, for instance, Jesse lost to Ralph Metcalfe in the 100 meters. In Bochum, Jesse's best long jump wasn't even half an inch more than 23 feet.

Jesse was tired—tired of traveling, tired of the competition, and tired of the AAU making money off his name when he couldn't even afford to buy his little girl a souvenir of the trip to Europe.

When the squad left London for a meet in Stockholm, Sweden—and eight more stops in Finland—Jesse was not with his teammates. He had stayed behind with Coach Snyder. Together, after conferring with NCAA officials, over whom the AAU had no power, they decided that Jesse was going home. They knew that could get him in trouble with the AAU, which needed him on the tour to satisfy promises they had made—not promises Jesse had made—to promoters.

As expected, the AAU was furious. But Jesse had never agreed to the grueling exhibition tour. That decision had been

Jesse is pictured while competing in the 4 × 100 meter relay in London during an exhibition tour following the Olympics. He has just taken the baton from teammate Marty Glickman.

made for him (as well as the other track Olympians) by the AAU. The AAU threatened action if Jesse didn't change his mind. He didn't.

On the day of the Closing Ceremonies of the Olympics—the track team's exhibition tour had begun even before the rest of the Games had wrapped up—U.S. Olympic Committee Chairman Avery Brundage and AAU Secretary-Treasurer Daniel Ferris announced that Jesse was suspended indefinitely. That meant he could not take part in any AAU-sanctioned meets—and that his amateur career effectively was over.

Jesse had done his best for his country. It was time to take care of himself—physically, emotionally, and financially. Even though he wouldn't necessarily be making money by running, Jesse knew it probably meant the end of his days as a Buckeye, too. The amateur rules in those days were much more strict than they are now.

Although it meant he would no longer have his star athlete on Ohio State's team, Coach Snyder approved of Jesse's decision. "It would be foolish for me to stand in Jesse's way," he said. "He's absolutely at the height of his fame now. Nothing he could do in his remaining year at college competition would lift him to a higher peak in the athletic world than he now enjoys."

Good Times and Bad

Jesse figured that nothing would stand in his way. "I'm the most famous person in the entire world," he later remembered thinking. He was the most famous sports personality, certainly. Upon Jesse's return to the United States after the Olympics, Cleveland held a parade in his honor. "By his high character, his clean living and attention to duty, he has brought this credit and honor to his Race, to this the greatest city of the world, to his alma mater, Ohio State, to our great commonwealth, to this country at large," the mayor exclaimed at a rally at City Hall.

Jesse, pictured with his wife, Ruth, received a hero's welcome upon returning to Cleveland in late August 1936.

Back in the United States following the Olympics, Jesse was the star attraction in a ticker-tape parade through the streets of New York.

Later on, there was a huge **ticker-tape parade** in New York City. Jesse sat in the front car with boxing champ Jack Dempsey.

Things were going well in Jesse's home life, too. His family was growing. Little Gloria soon was joined by two more daughters: Beverly, who was born in 1937, and Marlene, who was born in 1940.

Work possibilities seemed plentiful. Everyone wanted him to come work for their company, star in their movie, or endorse their candidate for political office—or so it seemed. For the most part, the offers were empty offers. One by one, the opportunities dried up. "It became increasingly apparent that everyone was going to slap me on the back," Jesse said. "But no one was going to offer me a job."

Entertainer Bill "Bojangles" Robinson was one of the few to stand by his overtures to Jesse. Robinson wanted Jesse to tour with him for a while.

Bojangles Robinson (1878–1949)

Bill "Bojangles" Robinson was an African American singer, dancer, and actor who was best known for his amazing tap-dancing skills.

Robinson, who was born in Richmond, Virginia, began making money as a dancer when he was just six years old. Before he was ten, he had dropped out of school to tour with a dance troupe.

Although he danced mostly for African American audiences until he was almost fifty years old, Bojangles eventually became extremely popular with white audiences as well. He began acting in motion pictures in the late 1920s, and is best known for appearing with child-star Shirley Temple in several films in the 1930s—although in a stereotyped African American role.

After Jesse Owens won his four gold medals in Berlin in 1936, Bojangles sent a telegram to the track star, telling him, "Don't do anything until you talk to me!" Jesse soon toured with Robinson, and the two grew to be close friends. "When Bill died, I lost a true friend," Jesse said.

Bojangles Robinson had a long and successful career as an entertainer, and was especially known for his tap dancing. This photograph was taken in the 1920s.

Alongside Bill "Bojangles" Robinson and other dancers, Jesse practices for the opening of a dance revue at the Cotton Club in New York City in September 1936.

Can't Keep a Good Man Down

Jesse was disappointed by so many empty promises. Many modern athletes, such as 2008 Olympic swimming star Michael Phelps, cash in on their Olympic glory almost from the moment they return home from the Games. But for Owens, it was much harder to find such reward on his return from Berlin.

For one thing, there was no steady way to make money in track and field. For another, the marketing of celebrities was different in Jesse's time than it is now. Certainly athletes were used to sell products, but the number of opportunities was far more limited then—even for someone as famous as Jesse Owens.

The other reality is that Jesse was an African American in a society that was still segregated—legally—in many ways. This was still nineteen years before African American Rosa Parks famously refused to give up her seat to a white passenger on a bus in Montgomery, Alabama.

"He was the idol of the country," Olympic teammate Marty Glickman said, "and a week later he was riding in the back of the bus."

In the sports world, there were few black stars. The budding National Football League had no African American players back then. Major-league baseball had an unofficial, but very real, color barrier. There was no National Basketball Association. Jesse and boxer Joe Louis were among the few African American sports heroes—at least among white fans.

Even President Franklin D. Roosevelt kept Jesse at arm's length after his amazing performance in the Olympics. "Hitler didn't snub me," Owens told an audience in Kansas City not long after the 1936 Games. "It was our president who snubbed me. The president didn't even send me a telegram."

It's possible that the president did not send any gold-medal-winning athletes any telegrams. It may not have been politically beneficial for Roosevelt to acknowledge Owens and other African American Olympians publicly because it "would have lost rather than gained him votes in the South." There was an election coming up in two months, and Roosevelt was mindful of the polls.

Things were not totally bleak, as Jesse sometimes portrayed them in his later years. There were times that he was reduced to running against horses in gimmick races or to working as a playground instructor—a job that he enjoyed because it allowed him to work with kids, but that paid little money—to make

Rosa Parks (1913–2005)

Historians point to December 1, 1955, as the birth date of the modern **civil-rights movement** in America. That was the day that Rosa Parks refused to give up her seat to a white passenger on a bus in Montgomery, Alabama.

At that time, it was still legal in some states to have separate facilities for whites and blacks, such as lunch counters or seating areas. Parks boarded a bus to head home from her job as a seamstress on the evening of December 1. When the bus driver asked her to move to make room for a white passenger, Parks refused. She was arrested and fined.

Parks's action, however, sparked the Montgomery Bus Boycott. The boycott lasted for more than a year as the courts decided the legality of Alabama's **segregation** laws for buses. In November 1956, the Supreme Court upheld a lower court's decision that the laws were unconstitutional. One month later, a new city ordinance allowed African Americans to sit anywhere they wished on the buses, and the boycott ended.

Parks died at age ninety-two in 2005. Her casket was placed in the rotunda of the United States Capitol for two days so that Americans could pay their respects. That's an honor usually reserved for former presidents of the United States; she was the first woman to lie in state—to be displayed publicly after death but before burial—at the Capitol.

After the United States Supreme Court ruled that Alabama's segregation rules for buses were illegal, Rosa Parks sat near the front of a bus in this photo from 1956. (A reporter is seated behind her.)

Sometimes, Jesse had to take part in gimmick races to help make ends meet. In this photo from 1948, he beats a horse to the finish line at Bay Meadows in the San Francisco area.

ends meet. But there were other times, too, like when he made enough money touring with Bojangles that he bought his parents a fifteen-room house in Cleveland. He bought Coach Riley a new car. Jesse was always very generous with his money.

For a while, Jesse made money in a dry-cleaning business, too, with a couple of partners. But then the business went bad and his partners skipped town, leaving him with a huge tax bill.

"But you can't keep a man like Jesse down," Ruth said.

He rebounded by working a variety of jobs. Many times, he was

In this photograph from 1954, Jesse talks with a customer in the drive-through area of his dry-cleaning business in Chicago.

Return of Riley

In 1960, the producers of a television show called *This Is Your Life* decided to honor Jesse Owens. For each episode *This Is Your Life* surprised a guest by inviting him or her to the studio for a reason other than being on the show. Meanwhile, Ralph Edwards, the host, and his staff secretly contacted friends and family to join the guest in reminiscing about memorable moments and events.

Jesse had been in on the secret a couple of times when the show honored other people that he knew. But this time, he was tricked into coming to the studio for a promotional video. One by one, many of the people who were important in Jesse's life were brought out, including an older sister, his wife, and Olympic teammates such as David Albritton and Ralph Metcalfe.

With the spotlight on him, Jesse seemed mostly embarrassed by all the attention. But when the producers brought out Riley, Jesse's eyes lit up. He had not seen his old coach, who by then was more than eighty years old, in almost fifteen years. The two shared a warm embrace, and recounted for the television audience some of their time together.

It turned out that would be the last time that Jesse ever saw his old coach. Riley died later that same year.

mentoring young people—much the way Coach Riley and Coach Snyder had mentored him.

Along with doing his many other post-Olympics jobs, Jesse helped administer a national physical-fitness program for the Civil Defense Office during World War II. (The United States was in the war from 1941 to its conclusion in 1945.) In the

During World War II, Jesse did work for the Civil Defense Office. In this photo, boxing champion Jack Dempsey stands beside a Civil Defense poster of Owens.

mid-1950s, he traveled overseas for the State Department during Dwight D. Eisenhower's tenure as president. Jesse was sent to places such as India, Malaysia, and the Philippines, where he trained athletes and talked at schools about the benefits of athletics, while fostering international friendship. He was called an "Ambassador of Sports."

Everyone in the world knew Jesse Owens from the 1936 Olympics, and they all wanted to hear what he had to say. "People always ask me about the 1936 Olympics," he once said. "But don't get me wrong. I'm glad they do it. If people forget about the Olympics, they forget what Hitler did there, and they forget about me."

As part of his work for the Eisenhower administration, Jesse traveled overseas. He's pictured in India in this photo from 1955.

CHAPTER 11

Death and Legacy

There will never be another athlete like Jesse Owens.

> —*Michael Johnson*

J esse spent much of the second half of his life going from city to city and meeting to meeting, giving speeches and pep talks. He was always on the move—just the way he liked it.

"Being in motion is what made running so natural to me," Jesse said, "those long hours and years of practice you have to put in—and want to put in—to become a champion. It was why, though I missed my family terribly at times, I felt natural in planes crossing oceans or trains traversing America . . . I hated to sit or to stand still."

In 1949, Jesse, Ruth, and their three daughters, Gloria, Beverly, and Marlene, all were on the move, relocating to Chicago. There, Jesse worked with the Chicago Boys' Club and the Illinois State Athletic Commission before really hitting his stride as a motivational speaker. Later, with their children grown, Jesse and Ruth moved to Arizona. Ruth wanted a quieter life there, but Jesse couldn't completely slow down. Most reports say he retired there. He still did some public-relations work, though, so he wasn't completely retired.

One day in 1979, Jesse complained of shortness of breath. He went to the doctor and was diagnosed with

Jesse initially struggled to find his niche after the 1936 Games, but then became a successful motivational speaker. He is pictured here late in his life, at age 65 in May 1979.

lung cancer. He had smoked a pack of cigarettes a day for more than thirty years, and it finally caught up with him. Not even Jesse could outrun that.

True to his nature, Jesse remained optimistic. Doctors, too, were hopeful of a recovery. They tried aggressive, advanced medical treatments. But Jesse was in and out of the hospital for the last several months of his life. He fell into a coma at the University of Arizona hospital on March 29, 1980. Ruth and their children rushed to his side, but it was too late. Jesse died two days later. He was sixty-six years old.

Still Famous

Nearly a quarter-century after his death, and more than three-quarters of a century after his brilliant athletic feats in

Germany, Jesse Owens's name is as famous as ever. Invariably, Olympic sprint champions every four years are still compared to him.

In 1984, American Carl Lewis set out to match Jesse's feat of winning four gold medals in the track competition of the Olympics, which were held that year in Los Angeles, California. Lewis not only earned four gold medals, but he also earned them in the same four events that Owens did: the 100 meters, 200 meters, long jump, and 4 × 100 meter relay.

Lewis never received the praise and recognition that Owens did, though. The politically charged atmosphere of Berlin was missing in Los Angeles (although the Soviet Union did boycott those Games in retaliation for the United States' boycott in 1980), but it was more than that. While the flamboyant Lewis was cocky and outspoken, Owens had been humble in victory and soft-spoken in manner.

> . . . *Owens had been humble in victory and soft-spoken in manner.*

After Lewis, no other man won both the 100 meters and 200 meters in the same Olympics until Jamaica's Usain Bolt did it in Beijing, China, in 2008. Bolt, who also ran a leg on Jamaica's gold-medal-winning 4 × 100 meter relay team, even set world records in both the 100 and the 200. But he spent the last several meters of the 100 pounding his chest and raising his arms—which was decidedly unlike Jesse Owens.

"That's not the way we perceive being a champion," International Olympic Committee President Jacques Rogge said.

Jesse, of course, learned early on from Coach Riley not to put on a show. Instead, his demeanor on the track was marked by sportsmanship and sincerity.

Jamaica's Usain Bolt exulted in drawing attention to himself while winning the 100 meters and the 200 meters in the 2008 Olympics. That was a marked contrast to the style of the humble and quiet Owens.

Role Model

That clearly was not just something Jesse took with him on the track, however. It was the way that he lived his life.

"He was a polite and humble man," veteran newspaperman Chuck Garrity, Sr., said. "The only trouble was getting more than one or two words out of him about himself. He didn't want to talk about himself."

"He was a remarkable person," said Louis Zamperini, a 1936 track Olympian in the 5,000 meters. "And he was a real gracious person. He had a very sweet nature about him."

"He wore his glory, I guess you might say, very gracefully," said Archie Williams, another American track star in 1936. "He wasn't cocky, but he was confident. He was just the kind of guy that you would want to be like. In fact, if anything, he was probably too nice, in that he would be the last one off the track, signing autographs and this and that, just very obliging."

Louis Zamperini

The son of Italian immigrants, Louis Zamperini (b. 1917) was a record-setting **miler** at Torrance (California) High School. He went on to the University of Southern California, where he competed on the Trojans' team that beat Jesse Owens and Ohio State for the 1935 NCAA championship. He made the 1936 Olympic Team in the 5,000 meters—although he placed eighth in the finals after gaining twelve pounds on the boat ride over to Berlin.

In 1943, Zamperini was lost at sea while flying a mission in World War II. After forty-seven days at sea, he was rescued by the Japanese navy and taken prisoner. He was held until the end of the war in 1945. In the meantime, he had been declared dead by the War Department.

Zamperini, with the help of Christian evangelist (preacher) Billy Graham, eventually became a motivational speaker. He now lives in Hollywood, California.

Lou Zamperini, standing behind the runners, is the starter for this race at New York City's Madison Square Garden in March 1946. Zamperini had been presumed dead during World War II.

In many ways, Jesse was like Booker T. Washington, the famous educator and African American leader. That's not a surprise. Jesse once said that Washington was his off-the-track idol, and that he wanted to be like him.

Today, nearly three-quarters of a century after Jesse's exploits in Berlin, many American track stars still want to be like him. "There will never be another athlete like Jesse Owens," four-time Olympic champion Michael Johnson said. Johnson cherishes a letter he once received from Jesse's wife, Ruth. In it, she told him that he was the runner who most reminded her of her husband.

Even non-track stars still look up to Owens. "Not only was he an amazing, well-rounded Olympic athlete, winning four gold medals in track and field, but he overcame such tremendous adversity," Olympic gymnast Dominique Moceanu once said. "He's a great inspiration as an athlete and as a role model."

American Hero

Long after Jesse's athletic career ended, major awards continued to pour in for him. In 1950, he was named the Associated Press's male track athlete for the first half of the twentieth century. In 1976, President Gerald Ford awarded him the Presidential Medal of Freedom. Fourteen years later, Jesse posthumously (after death) was awarded the Congressional Gold Medal by President George

In 1990, President George H. W. Bush presented Ruth Owens with a Congressional Gold Medal in Jesse's name. Jesse was honored for his "humanitarian contributions in the race of life."

Booker T. Washington (1856–1915)

Booker T. Washington was an influential African American author, orator, and leader of the black community. Most of all, though, he was an educator. He advocated education as the means for African Americans to achieve true equality in the post-slavery days in the United States.

Washington was born a slave in Franklin County, Virginia, in 1856. He was nine years old when the Thirteenth Amendment officially ended slavery. Like Jesse Owens, Washington supported working with whites to combat prejudice. Neither man saw violence as a means to achieving civil rights. Both men had critics among civil-rights advocates who felt their views were too appeasing.

Washington was the first head of the Tuskegee Institute in Alabama in 1881, where many former slaves not only learned to read and write but also built the campus as an indication of self-reliance.

This photograph of Booker T. Washington was taken in the late 1890s or early 1900s. Jesse Owens's philosophies about race relations were much in line with those of the famous African American educator.

Presidential Medal of Freedom

The Presidential Medal of Freedom is the nation's highest civilian honor. It is awarded by the president of the United States to individuals who have made "an especially meritorious contribution to (1) the security or national interests of the United States, or (2) world peace, or (3) cultural, or other significant public or private endeavors."

The award was first given during World War II as a way for President Harry Truman to honor civilian contributions to that effort. In the 1960s, President John F. Kennedy brought back the award and expanded its range. It now honors people in areas as varied as politics, sports, religion, business, art, and entertainment. Past recipients include people such as civil-rights activist Martin Luther King, Jr., former president Ronald Reagan, humanitarian Mother Teresa, the astronauts and crew members of the *Apollo 13* Mission Operations Team, artist Georgia O'Keeffe, actress Lucille Ball, actor John Wayne, singer Frank Sinatra, television newscaster Walter Cronkite, and Pope John Paul II.

H. W. Bush. In 1996, the Jesse Owens Memorial Park, complete with a museum honoring his legendary accomplishments, opened in Oakville, Alabama. Just a few days after the park was completed, the Olympic Torch arrived en route to Atlanta for the 1996 Games.

It is more than Jesse's athletic accomplishments, of course, that make his name still resonate with Americans today. It is the enduring notion that in Berlin in 1936, Jesse represented the forces of good against the forces of evil. And the forces of good won.

These children are pictured on a tour of the Jesse Owens Museum in 2008. The museum is part of the Jesse Owens Memorial Park in Oakville, Alabama.

Today's media are quick to call athletes "heroes." But hitting the game-winning home run, or scoring a record-setting touchdown, or even winning four gold medals in the Olympics—while certainly thrilling and perhaps admirable—is neither courageous nor heroic. Jesse Owens's performance at the 1936 Games, however, went beyond athletics.

His gold-medal winning efforts—and the high character, class, and dignity with which he performed—remain a symbol in stark contrast to Adolf Hitler and Nazi Germany. Jesse's performance in the face of such adversity was indeed heroic.

Glossary

abolish—put an end to something, such as a law.

archrival—biggest enemy in athletic competition.

Aryans—white people of non-Jewish descent.

bigotry—treating members of a particular group, especially a racial or ethnic group, with hatred or intolerance.

boosters—men and women who support a school's athletic program with their time or money.

boycott—refuse to take part in something as a protest for an organization's action, or to get that organization to change its actions.

civil-rights movement—in the United States, the political movement for equality for African Americans; it is generally considered to have lasted from 1955 to 1968.

Communist—a political doctrine in which the government controls the means of production and ownership of property.

conjecture—guesswork.

formidable—difficult to beat.

fraternity—a social organization, typically of men in college.

fundamentals—the basic skills on which other skills are built.

mentor—an advisor or teacher.

miler—an athlete that competes in a one-mile race.

NAACP—an influential civil-rights organization in the United States; founded in 1909, its stated mission is to "ensure the political, educational, social, and economic equality of rights of all persons and to eliminate racial hatred and racial discrimination."

newsreel—a short movie, shown in theaters before or after films, about current events.

page—someone, usually a young person, employed to deliver messages and run errands for lawmakers.

promoter—a person who takes on the financial responsibilities of a sporting event and arranges for the participants.

propaganda—the spread of information or ideas to further a particular cause; often considered deceptive.

regime—the government of a particular country, especially one that is considered to be oppressive.

segregation—the separation of people of different races, classes, or ethnic groups for reasons of prejudice.

socialites—prominent members of society who regularly are in the news for entertaining or being entertained by others of a similar social standing.

stock market—a place where stocks, or portions of publicly owned companies, are bought and sold.

tailwind—a wind heading in the same direction as an object in movement, in this case an athlete; a strong tailwind can help a runner or jumper go faster or farther.

ticker-tape parade—a parade through city streets in which paper ribbons often are thrown from office windows in celebration of the honoree; ticker tape was the paper on which a telegraph printed its information.

varsity—the highest level of team play at a school.

Bibliography

Books

Baker, William J. *Jesse Owens: An American Life.* New York: The Free Press, 1986.

Coe, Sebastian, and Nicholas Mason. *The Olympians.* London: Pavilion Books, 1984.

Hart-Davis, Duff. *Hitler's Games.* New York: Harper & Row, 1986.

Large, David Clay. *Nazi Games: The Olympics of 1936.* New York: W. W. Norton and Co., 2007.

Owens, Jesse. *Jesse: The Man Who Outran Hitler.* With Paul Neimark New York: Fawcett Gold Medal, 1978.

Schaap, Jeremy. *Triumph.* New York: Mariner Books, 2007.

Wallechinsky, David. *The Complete Book of the Summer Olympics.* Toronto: SportClassic Books, 2004.

Walters, John. *Sports in America: 1920–1939.* New York: Facts on File, Inc., 2004.

Articles

Associated Press. "IOC Blasts Bolt: Not the Way We Perceive Being a Champion." nbcolympics.com, August 21, 2008.

Associated Press. "Offers Indicate That Jesse Owens Might Become Pro." *Galveston Daily News,* August 10, 1936.

Bock, Hal. "Old Olympians Salute Jesse Owens." Associated Press Archive, December 17, 1999.

Brauner, Dale with Charles Curtis. "Over Time With Sports and Protest." *ESPN Magazine,* July 15, 2008.

Gould, Alan. "Jesse Owens Leads American Advances." *Galveston Daily News.* August 5, 1936.

Holland, Debbie. "Michael Johnson Tells How Legacy of Jesse Owens Inspired Him to Olympic Double Gold." *Jet,* August 26, 1996.

International News Service. "New Record for Casting Shot." *Van Wert Daily Bulletin,*
    August 22, 1932.

Jones, Todd. "A Good Day's Work." *Columbus Dispatch,* May 25, 2005.

LuValle, James E., Archie F. Williams, and Louis S. Zamperini, all interviewed by
    George A. Hodak. Amateur Athletic Foundation Olympian's Oral Histories, 1988.

New York Daily News. "The Regret of a Lifetime." February 2, 2003.

Pardys, Sara. Interview with Dominique Moceanu. "In Pictures: Olympians Pick the
    Perfect Athlete." Forbes.com, July 8, 2008.

Pierson, Don. "Jesse Owens: Hero for the Ages." *Chicago Tribune,* April 1, 1980.

Web Sites

George Bush Presidential Library and Museum Web site: http://bushlibrary.tamu.edu/
    research/public_papers.php?id=1701&year=1990&month=3

Jesse Owens: Olympic Legend: www.jesseowens.com

Jesse Owens Museum: www.jesseowensmuseum.org

LA84 Foundation: www.la84foundation.org

Library of Congress: American Memory: http://memory.loc.gov/ammem/index.html

Official Web Site of the Olympic Movememt: www.olympic.org

Olympics Statistics and History: www.sports-reference.com/olympics

Presidential Medal of Freedom Executive Order 11085: http://www.lib.umich.edu/
    govdocs/jfkeo/eo/11085.htm

Video

Olympia: The Leni Riefenstahl Archival Collection, DVD. Directed by Leni Riefenstahl.
    Venice, CA: Pathfinder Home Entertainment, 2006.

This Is Your Life Ultimate Collection, DVD. Directed by Axel Gruenberg and Richard
    Gottlieb. Portland, OR: R2 Entertainment, 2005.

Interview

Garrity, Chuck. Interview with the author, July 2008.

Source Notes

The following citations list the sources of quoted material in this book. The first and
last few words of each quotation are cited and followed by their source. Complete
information on referenced sources can be found in the Bibliography.

Abbreviations:
AAF—Amateur Athletic Foundation Olympian's Oral Histories
AI—Author Interview
GBL—George Bush Presidential Library and Museum Web site
GDW—"A Good Day's Work"

GDN—"Offers Indicate That Jesse Owens Might Become Pro"

HG—*Hitler's Games*

INS—International News Service, August 22, 1932

IP—"In Pictures: Olympians Pick the Perfect Athlete"

JO—*Jesse: The Man Who Outran Hitler*

JOAL—*Jesse Owens: An American Life*

JOHA—"Jesse Owens: Hero for the Ages"

JOL—"Jesse Owens Leads American Advances"

JOM—www.jesseowensmuseum.org

JOWS—www.jesseowens.com

LOC—Library of Congress: "American Memory"

MJ—"Michael Johnson Tells How Legacy of Jesse Owens Inspired Him to Olympic Double Gold"

NG—*Nazi Games: The Olympics of 1936*

OOS—"Old Olympians Salute Jesse Owens"

OTW—"Over Time With Sports and Protest"

PMF—Presidential Medal of Freedom, Executive Order 11085

TIYL—*This Is Your Life*

TRI—*Triumph*

TRL— "The Regret of a Lifetime"

INTRODUCTION: Good Versus Evil

PAGE 1 *"Finally he was . . . competing against Hitler.":* TRI, p. 216

PAGE 1 *"He had gone to Berlin . . . competing against Hitler.":* TRI, p. 216

CHAPTER 1: Humble Beginnings

PAGE 2 *"I always loved running . . . courage of your own lungs.":* JO, p. 24

PAGE 2 *"gift child.":* JOAL, p. 7

PAGE 7 *"I'm going to take the bump out now, J. C.,":* JO, p. 12

PAGE 7 *"Real pain is . . . because it wouldn't help.":* JO, p. 12

PAGE 7 *"I was only five years old, but I knew I was dying,":* JO, p. 13

PAGE 7 *"Pray, James Cleveland. Pray.":* JO, p. 16

PAGE 7 *"gift child":* JOAL, p. 7

PAGE 9 *"We used to have . . . Who had steak?":* JOWS

PAGE 9 *"I always loved running . . . your own lungs.":* JO, p. 24

CHAPTER 2: Northern Exposure

PAGE 11 *"It's gonna . . . to a better life.":* JO, p. 29

PAGE 11 *"belongings together and . . . on a train,":* JO, p. 28

PAGE 11 *"I told them the opportunities were better there,":* TIYL

PAGE 12 *"We'd never make it. We'd starve.":* JO, p. 26

PAGE 12 *"And where's the train . . . to a better life,":* JO, p. 29

PAGES 13–14 *"What is your name? . . .Yes, ma'am,":* TIYL

PAGE 16 *"best baby-sitter I ever had,":* TIYL

PAGE 17 *"I fell in . . . we ever talked,":* JO, p. 38

CHAPTER 3: Coach and Mentor

PAGE 20 *"If this lad . . . the Olympics someday.":* TIYL

PAGE 20 *"How'd you like . . . to high school?":* JO, p. 39

Image Credits

About the Author

Jim Gigliotti is a freelance writer who lives in Southern California with his wife and two children. He has written more than thirty books on sports and personalities for youngsters. A former editor at National Football League Publishing, his writing credits also include *Stadium Stories: USC Trojans, Obsessed with Football,* and *Obsessed with Baseball.*

Index

Discover interesting personalities
in the Sterling Biographies® series:

Muhammad Ali: *King of the Ring*

Marian Anderson: *A Voice Uplifted*

Neil Armstrong: *One Giant Leap for Mankind*

Alexander Graham Bell: *Giving Voice to the World*

Cleopatra: *Egypt's Last and Greatest Queen*

Christopher Columbus: *The Voyage That Changed the World*

Jacques Cousteau: *A Life Under the Sea*

Davy Crockett: *Frontier Legend*

Marie Curie: *Mother of Modern Physics*

Frederick Douglass: *Rising Up from Slavery*

Amelia Earhart: *A Life in Flight*

Thomas Edison: *The Man Who Lit Up the World*

Albert Einstein: *The Miracle Mind*

Anne Frank: *Hidden Hope*

Benjamin Franklin: *Revolutionary Inventor*

Lou Gehrig: *Iron Horse of Baseball*

Matthew Henson: *The Quest for the North Pole*

Harry Houdini: *Death-Defying Showman*

Thomas Jefferson: *Architect of Freedom*

Joan of Arc: *Heavenly Warrior*

Helen Keller: *Courage in Darkness*

John F. Kennedy: *Voice of Hope*

Martin Luther King, Jr.: *A Dream of Hope*

Lewis & Clark: *Blazing a Trail West*

Abraham Lincoln: *From Pioneer to President*

Jesse Owens: *Gold Medal Hero*

Rosa Parks: *Courageous Citizen*

Jackie Robinson: *Champion for Equality*

Eleanor Roosevelt: *A Courageous Spirit*

Franklin Delano Roosevelt: *A National Hero*

Babe Ruth: *Legendary Slugger*

Jim Thorpe: *An Athlete for the Ages*

Harriet Tubman: *Leading the Way to Freedom*

George Washington: *An American Life*

The Wright Brothers: *First in Flight*

Malcolm X: *A Revolutionary Voice*